The Friend

Finding Compassion with Yourself

First published by O Books, 2010
O Books is an imprint of John Hunt Publishing Ltd., The Bothy, Deershot Lodge, Park Lane, Ropley,
Hants, SO24 0BE, UK
office1@o-books.net
www.o-books.net

Distribution in:

UK and Europe
Orca Book Services
orders@orcabookservices.co.uk
Tel: 01202 665432 Fax: 01202 666219   Int.
code (44)

USA and Canada
NBN
custserv@nbnbooks.com
Tel: 1 800 462 6420 Fax: 1 800 338 4550

Australia and New Zealand
Brumby Books
sales@brumbybooks.com.au
Tel: 61 3 9761 5535 Fax: 61 3 9761 7095

Far East (offices in Singapore, Thailand,
Hong Kong, Taiwan)
Pansing Distribution Pte Ltd
kemal@pansing.com
Tel: 65 6319 9939 Fax: 65 6462 5761

South Africa
Stephan Phillips (pty) Ltd
Email: orders@stephanphillips.com
Tel: 27 21 4489839 Telefax: 27 21 4479879

Text copyright Nishant Matthews 2009

Design: Stuart Davies

ISBN: 978 1 84694 271 6

A CIP catalogue record for this book is available
from the British Library.

Printed by Digital Book Print

O Books operates a distinctive and ethical publishing philosophy in
all areas of its business, from its global network of authors to
production and worldwide distribution.

The Friend

Finding Compassion with Yourself

Nishant Matthews

BOOKS

Winchester, UK
Washington, USA

Contents

Acknowledgements

The Friend is a work of co-operation. The deep inspiration comes from Osho, my spiritual master. Standing nearby is Chogyam Trungpa, the Tibetan master. I hold both in deep gratefulness to their impeccable authenticity and rebellious spirit. There is further support here from A.H. Almaas, especially in the area of bridging daily experience with religious aspiration.

In the writing, Pavitra Wolf offered deep personal support and clear editorial guidance. Komala Lyra gave very welcome insight to the writing and organization.

Mattie Pragya of Denmark contributed the artwork.

Claus Devayan Henriksen, also of Denmark, is the photographer whose work appears on the cover, as well as the author's photograph.

Madhurima Rigtrup's (Denmark) work with the "intelligent heart" has also been a personal support and inspiration.

Rob Gras of Amsterdam provided personal guidance as well as early commentary for the manuscript.

Nutan Peeters of Haarlem has also contributed to this work both with personal support and research into Mary.

Solvei Lundmark of Sweden and her Fonebo team provided the friendship and a setting where much of the book's research could happen.

There is also a nameless one who brought me into this project some years ago, and has led me along its way ever since.

I would also like to thank my family, Scott Matthews, Elizabeth Brunt, and Bebe Matthews for their background support and friendship through this. Corky Pollard deserves a special mention in this list as well.

Finally, a special thank you to the Dutch Rebalancing Opleiding for its gracious hospitality to the evolution of the

Acknowledgements

Friend work. Danke je Rob, Jeanine, Wilko, Erica, Alice, Mariska, Inge, Marriet, Ellie, Tineke, Barabara and the other friends there.

For further information about The Friend as a way of living
please visit the website
www.BodyandBeyond.nl

Zen Buddhism and western psychotherapy are currently merging in the West much as Buddhism and Taoism did in ancient China to form Zen as we know it today. Zen allows us to experience true emptiness and no-self; psychotherapy provides tools to discover the disowned aspects of our selves that act out in underhanded, covert and even perverted ways. Zen offers probably the deepest and most profound understanding of our true self; psychotherapy helps us become healthier self-actualizing individuals. Together they can enable us to include and yet transcend self and no-self and live life as the unique and true self.

I recommend The Friend *as a good guide book for such journeys and understanding.*

Zen Master Dennis Genpo Merzel, author of *Big Mind Big Heart, Finding Your Way*

Finally an emotionally intelligent guide for all of us who seek to befriend ourselves and others in the process.

Nishant Matthews offers us an extremely powerful (yet never invasive) wise and inspiring way to come to understand our body, heart and soul, and how they work together.

The Friend is at the same time an extraordinarily readable journal of a quest for our universal oneness and eternal innocence.

Caroline Beumer-Peeters, co-author of *Parents' Skills* (a guide for solution focused parenting based on "Kids' Skills"), co-author of the Dutch version of *Mission Possible* and author of "*Mission Possible, Manual for Coaches*"

The Friend provides a bridge between our personal self and our True Nature — uniting and honoring both aspects of our experience as human beings. In this book Nishant shows us how to cross that bridge without sacrificing either shore.

Regardless of where you are in your journey of awakening, the wisdom and compassion in The Friend *will delight your heart and make your journey easier. You will want to share it with your Friends!*

Rhea Powers, author of *A Call to the Lightworkers*

The Friend is written from the unique perspective of a therapist with a wealth of experience involving eastern and western psychological and spiritual disciplines. The wisdom and practical experience Nishant brings, as evidenced in the dialogues with clients, illustrates powerfully this truly transformative work. To practice love, trust, and gratitude towards oneself opens a journey back to oneself that I found inspiring, challenging, and liberating. This book is a major contribution to the frontiers in exploring and evolving our consciousness.

Larry Wallace, O.D., Ph.D., President of the College of Syntonic Optometry, President of the International Light Association

I absolutely love your book. It is packed with wisdom. You have the talent to make something very complicated so simple and easy to understand. That is a gift. And you do it with so a wonderful touch of love and light.

I love the way you also put a new perspective to why we create the ego and what it actually is. I feel there is so much truth in this book, so much important knowledge that people all over the world would benefit from. And it is told in such an embracing way!

Sagar Bohnstedt author of *Living Between*

Preface

There is a world of experience that most of us know well. This is the familiar world of our normal self, "me," the person we are with our thoughts and feelings and dreams and fears and hopes.

There is also another world that many of us have experienced from time to time. This is the world of grace. In grace there is something bigger and steadier than the "me" that we normally live in. I call that bigger something Being or True Nature.

While our normal sense of me has size, shape, age, history, thoughts, and feelings, in True Nature the experience of self is radically different. There is a gut level sense of harmony. In that harmony, our age and size expand far beyond our present body. We are big, timeless, and very at home with our self. We also sense that the self we are is not living in isolation, that actually our expanded body eventually merges into something bigger than us. We sense a larger field around us, and that we have a place in this field that is both vast and personal. We experience delight in the abundant, clean energy of this world of Being.

In time we are likely to discover its intelligence and kindness as well. While the normal self works hard for its happiness, in the world of Being happiness appears spontaneously, as natural as the sun rising every morning.

While it seems that these two worlds are very separate from each other, actually they co-exist. Even though the experience of the two is radically different, the reality is the world of Being exists within the familiar world of personal limitation.

The Friend is a bridge between the two worlds. It offers a way of being with our personal, daily experience where the grace of our being and the efforts of our personality are intimately linked. The Friend's way is of learning to be with our selves in such a way that the grace within us is encouraged and supported to emerge, take its place in our psyche, and manifest its truth

1

in the world.

In many years of working with people in Australia, Japan, China, USA, and Europe, I've come to appreciate how rare it is for any of us to have deep, nourishing contact with ourselves.

While most of us have heard, "The answer lies within," and are sincere in our intention to "know thyself," what happens in daily life is never so simple. In fact, there is an almost aversion to being with our self. It seems like there is some mistake going on; that the self that we are today can't be who we are supposed to be. The way we are here and now doesn't appear grand and good and full of mystery and meaning. The sad truth is that even morning TV appears more interesting than simply hanging out with our self. The guy who we are right now can't be what Buddha and Socrates had in mind when they suggested we look inside. In fact, the self that is here today seems to be more part of the problem than part of the solution.

It doesn't seem to matter much where we come from or how good or bad our lives are, most of us still carry a deep inner conviction of deficiency, that "there is something wrong with me." We have the idea true goodness must be somewhere other than in our self. Maybe it is in God or some hero or someone we love or in our kids…

The Friend invites God out of the sky and the hero out of the past. It says these things must be here in each of us also. They are not confined to people of magical birth. Grace is part of all of us. And, as grace is part of all of us, how we can be with our self in a way that the Grace inside us becomes a part of our experience? How to be with our normal experience in a way that the underlying reality of True Nature comes through even when we are not at our best or even close?

The way of the Friend unfolds through learning kindness to our own experience. In that kindness are the seeds of understanding. When we bring kindness and a willingness to listen and understand the self, that same self responds graciously.

2

My wish is that the Friend's grace will be a natural part of everyone's daily experience.

Overview

Part One: The Way of the Friend

Part one introduces the Friend as a way of seeing and relating with ourselves.

Part Two: The Journey Within

The second part of the book is about contact between the "I" that we know and the self that is within. It follows a sequence of developing self understanding that is based on the Tibetan tradition of awakening to our True Nature. In this sequence, we discover the Earth (Ice), Water, Fire, and Air (Space) elements within our selves. Each of these elements represents aspects of our consciousness. As we encounter these different aspects, we are challenged to learn new lessons. Through this progression we are taken into more intimate contact with our True Nature.

As we follow this path, we recover more and more of our real self. We find a new fullness in being who we are, a new sense of adventure in discovering our way in daily life. We recover a deep goodness inside ourselves, and in that deep goodness are many fine gifts, the unique qualities of our own soul.

Part Three: Experiential Training

The third part of the book offers practical skills for recovering and enhancing contact within ourselves. You will learn heart skills and simple ways to mature the inner relating. Included in this section are examples of sessions in groups and individual counseling.

Part Four: Separation and Returning

The last part of the book is for professionals or those who want an advanced understanding of the separation between normal self and True Nature. It portrays the conditioning process that takes us out of the garden of the self and into the wilderness of self control and self rejection and knowing our self only through the reflections we get from other people. It shows the process in which the created self comes to stand before the True Self.

Introduction

Inside each of us is a core of living goodness. Actually, to even say goodness is too small a label. Inside us is a wellspring of consciousness that has a seemingly endless capacity to reveal beauty, grace, intelligence, humor, joy and more. This inner core is recognized as our True Nature by the many people who have managed to find it.

When our eyes and hearts are open, this is not so difficult to see in others. It is there in our children's smile, our lover's glance, and even in the way the dog runs to greet us when we come home. We can find it in a winter's snowflake and a summer's sunset wave coming into the beach.

Knowing the goodness around us is not so difficult, but when it comes to knowing it in our selves, it is a different story. While we might think about our goodness or hear others talk about it from time to time, we hardly experience this goodness in a tangible way. For most of us, our inner core is as far away and as mysterious as God Himself.

Not knowing what is really at our core, we look elsewhere for guidance and confirmation.

What we do know is a self. This self has a very familiar feeling to it. We know its moods, its thoughts, its feelings and its history. We know what it likes and what it doesn't like. With a little intro-spection, we know its good points and its bad ones. When it gets what it wants, we are happy, and when it doesn't, then we aren't so happy.

We try to be happy by making this self happy. Even as we gather enormous resources around us to make ourselves happy, staying happy is a slippery affair. With a little attention, we see that the happiness that comes from the outside is a very fickle friend. Trying to secure this kind of happiness leads us to be very busy. We have many things to do and many people to please and not much protection from the self criticism that comes with all this being busy.

As we become more consumed with our self, we lose track of our Being.

We come to live in a world where the natural goodness is lost. We become addicted to a created self and its created joys and sorrows, missions and accomplishments.

The Friend is an invitation to journey into and through our created selves so that we can reunite with the original self, our True Nature. The way of the Friend's journey is through heartful intimacy with all the aspects of our self—good or not. In the Friend's warmth and understanding, we recover a magical kind of intimacy within our self. We find the self will communicate with us, and, as we learn its ways, it will relax its rigidity and controls. In that relaxation we are invited into deeper levels of our self, the places where the created self and the Being are more clearly co-existing. As we come into these places with a Friend's awareness, the created self finds a new relationship with the original self. True Nature, once recognized, begins a dance of unfolding and flowing through the created self. There is a sense of coming home, of finding inner Presence, of waking up to something both original and precious inside us.

Turning In

Late one evening, the whole village wakens to the sounds out in the street. An old, wise Sufi woman named Rabia is on her hands and knees scouring the street for something, and as she looks around she mutters to herself in between cries and moans of anguish.

Because she is beloved in the village, many people come out to join her on her search.

In the torch light and candle light, they also get down on their hands and knees and look at the cobblestones for the sewing needle Rabia has lost. After an hour, nearly all the adults in the village are gathered around, when one of them says, "Rabia, we have searched and

7

searched but we are not finding your needle anywhere. Can you tell us exactly where it is that you lost it?"

Rabia stands up and says, "I lost it in my house."

Everyone is shocked. They also stand up. "Then why are we looking for it out here on the street?"

"Because," says Rabia, "My house is so dark I didn't think I could find it in there, so I came out here to the street where there is more light."

"Beloved Rabia," said one of the neighbors, "We have wondered if you are wise or crazy all these years, but now…this is too much. How can you explain calling all of us out here like this?"

Rabia smiled. "You have called me crazy for years, but what can I say of you? I at least know where to go to find myself while you keep searching for yourselves out in the streets and in the crowds, and you never go inside your own house to find who is in."[1]

The quest for finding our True Self starts its long germination process in the dark. Like Rabia's villagers, we start from a place of looking outside for something that can only be found inside. From being outside of True Nature, we don't really know what is in there, and in the rare moments when we do meet it, often we don't know if it angel or demon. Only in the totality of the meeting can we find out. Going even a little way into personal reality confronts us with fear, sadness, anger, hate, withdrawal, love, peace, gratitude, serenity and more. Are they angels? Demons? Are we good? Are we bad? In the dark of the inner world, we don't really know until we take the time and make the effort to meet and feel and discover what our self is offering us.

Many thousands of people have realized how daunting the inner world is, and many disciplines, religions, philosophies and therapies have been created in response. The Friend's way stands in this tradition. The Friend's way is birthed in a time when it is called for. It speaks a contemporary language and uses all the contemporary tools available for connecting with the reality that is both within and without.

In the Friend's way, our inner world has its psychological architecture. This architecture has its patterns and its logic. By understanding these, we can go inside ourselves deeply and gracefully. With a little inner light, we come to see that our inner architecture is made as a psycho-dynamic system of protection. The barriers inside are there with the purpose of protecting us from some painful things we experienced in the past. With a clear understanding of how we create a psycho-dynamic system of protection, we can navigate to the inner core of our True Nature. This is like having an understanding of how our house is built, and which doors need keys and which doors can open by hand.

In many of the older traditions, there has been no such understanding of our inner psychological architecture. Belief was supposed to guide us and protect us when the going got tough. Belief and magic were substitutes for personal experience, especially the kind that leads to direct knowing of grace. Even in the meditative traditions, going inside meant going into a dark strange house without many keys. In this kind of approach, one meets many obstacles that appear to be barriers between the seeker and the inner being. What to do with pride, anger, sadness, sexuality, hopelessness…the living stuff of our inner world? In the older traditions, the inner world holds many things which had to be fought, destroyed, abandoned or simply watched for thirty years. The religious seekers had only a few of the resources now available. Some doors opened, and many did not.

When we don't have a key, a door feels like a wall. We take it as a barrier and we break it or retreat. Since the inner doors are our own constructions, there is immense frustration in beating against the doors of our own protection systems. We are fighting our selves, and in that fight, we usually lose. However, when we do have keys and understanding, a door is a passageway. It opens to even a gentle touch, and allows us to go further inside our inner architecture. The door is simply a small challenge that protects something valuable inside. With the right keys and the right approach, the doors of our inner world gratefully swing open and invite us into a deeper participation with True Nature.

In the Friend's approach, the inner doors open to the heart quality of those who knock on it. When we can meet our inner barriers with heartfulness, intelligence, fearlessness, curiosity, understanding, compassion, and sensitivity, then our doors willingly open. The same anger, fear, pride, sexuality that were barriers to going inside can also graciously allow us to pass through when we greet them properly. If, on the other hand, we meet our inner demons with fear, rejection, hostility, judgment, blame, and separation, then our doors remain shut.

To a critical, judging mind our inner being doesn't reveal itself. Our inner self is naturally protective and elusive when it senses criticism and danger, even from us. Equally naturally, our inner self responds generously when it is heartfully addressed.

This book is dedicated to restoring the Friend quality within our selves. A friend accepts and invites us to be who we are. In good friendship, we feel seen, heard, recognized, encouraged, and loved for what we have to offer. Friends naturally bring out the best in each other. Just as we can offer and receive friendship with others, we can also learn this art within our self.

In the light of the inner friend, it is easy to recover our ability to be intimate with our self, to allow and encourage our unique being to unfold. *The Friend* offers practical skills to bring wholesome attention within, to offer to our self the quality of attention that will encourage the Inner One to reveal and grow. Along the way, this book offers sensible, compassionate under-standing to the state of separation we have inside. It teaches a way of seeing that brings clarity and love.

The Friend invites us to recover what seems to have been lost.

Part One

The Way of the Friend

The Friend

Friendliness is really an attitude, a way of relating to ourselves and the world around us. It is the click, that quality of warm clarity that somehow recognizes who we are and welcomes us as we are.

Being friends with others brings us love; being friends with our selves brings reunion. In such reunion we reconnect with what has been forgotten inside.

It begins with a willingness to look, to reflect our attention back towards our self. Looking at our self would seem to be so frequent and so easy that one could wonder why even mention it at all. However, in personal experience we can quickly find that this first step is one of the most difficult. We don't look at our self very easily or, for that matter, very deeply. We might see the wrinkles on the skin or the way our hair is combed, but we don't sit easy with the sadness in the eyes or the tiredness across the shoulders. At first glance, we are not likely to find much comfort and joy in bringing a mirror back to our self. In fact, there is likely to be aversion to who we find in there, if we find anyone at all. The way in which we look at our selves is often dark or cold or clouded with pride. Our personal mirror holds so many memories in it that we can hardly see who is here today.

With a little practice, we realize the One who looks doesn't have an easy communication with the One who is seen. The One who is seen often is judged, misunderstood, and, worst insult of all, ignored by the one who looks. The communication levels between the two are rigid, often frozen. The self feels both hurt and antagonistic to the separated judging consciousness that approaches it.

In *The Friend* we learn to hold the mirror firmly and see what reflects back to us. We realize that without kindness, we will never really know who is in that mirror. We also will realize that this deep level kindness doesn't come easy. Can we offer warm eyes to the one we see in the mirror? Can we dare to see into that mirror with courage and understanding and compassion?

The miracle of kindness is communication. When we bring kindness to the one we see inside, he/she begins communicating back with us. If we can be heartful with what is being communicated to us, then our inner doors open and we are invited even deeper into the Self where even more will be communicated.

As we gain confidence, the ability to look inside takes us on an inner journey. It shows us things, many of which we won't like. If we react to those things harshly, then our inner world retreats from us and becomes like a desert in the glare of a burning sun. That inner harshness is in all of us. It acts as though it knows who we should be, how we should feel, why we should perform. This inner judge withers whatever it contacts. It makes life inside our selves so unpleasant that most of us will do anything to avoid it.

There is an old story of Alexander the Great meeting the Indian mystic fakir Diogenes. Diogenes was lying naked in the sun by the bank of the river. Alexander was impressed with Diogenes' peacefulness, and asked how he could have these things for himself. Diogenes said, "Simple. Take off all that armor and relax here in the sun with me." Alexander had conquered everything in his path, but to simply sit down and be quiet was too challenging for him. He felt naked taking off his armor, and even more naked to simply sit in the sun and abandon the driving ambition that had guided him all of his life. Alexander replied lamely that he would when he came back in a few years time after he had conquered the rest of the world.

In the story, even Alexander realized the irony of the situation: fearless in conquering the world, technically he owned most of the civilized world, but just to hang out with himself in innocent nakedness was too scary. His Greatness outside offered him no protection against what he would face inside.

Even Alexander the Great, conqueror of everything from Greece to India, was in the same boat as the rest of us: fear of self. This fear of self is an earned phenomenon; when we relate to our selves from separation, criticism, and the many practices that separate us, the self appears alien and hostile. The inner doors stay shut. We lose contact with the simple goodness of the self, and go seeking it somewhere else. Because the inner pathways are not available, we look outside. We try to recover our sense of goodness through our relationships, our work, our religion, our creativity and so on. Doing this has its moments, but basically never really works at the level we need it to work. We can have many trophies, certificates, and confirmations hanging on the wall and still feel empty inside. Ask Alexander.

There are many ways to meet our selves. From a place of Ignorance, we can order ourselves around; alternatively we can collapse with the demands of the self. We can give in to our fears and desires. We can embark on self-improvement programs. We can fear ourself, blame ourself, be proud of ourself, criticize ourself...the list of unproductive ways to be with the self is endless. Often these unproductive exchanges with the self are frustrating and demoralizing.

The more productive ways combine a sense of warm understanding with clear awareness. For this, *The Friend* combines Western Psychology with Eastern meditation.

Western psychology brings understanding into the way we develop as people. It gives us a sense of context, a sense of history. When we really understand how we are made and the forces that shaped us, it is easier to open our heart to our situation. The understanding brings a caring, a sense of wanting to support the development of this self with all its struggles and issues. We realize that we are a work in progress and we can see the past of where we have come from and the potential futures that we are heading for.

Eastern meditation, on the other hand, brings a different

dimension of consciousness, a dimension of awareness. Awareness is the ability to be present with a non-reactive state of mind. It is the quality of seeing intelligence that is honed through meditation. Awareness invites us into the experience of no-time, and no-history. We meet the self as though we are meeting it for the very first time. Because awareness is something that exists out of time, it brings the eyes of innocence to what it sees. With the eyes of innocence it appreciates the innocence that it discovers in the self. Awareness allows us to innocently approach our self and to stand in respect to the innocence of the self that opens to us.

In *The Friend* the combination of psychological understanding with meditative awareness gives us the keys to go inside. In the depth of the self we find many challenges, especially the challenges of the denied or dis-owned shadow self. We find our fears, our grief, our insecurity, our greed, or sirens of delusion, our self criticism…and more. When we can meet these challenges with understanding and awareness, we realize that we can meet these parts of our self without shame or fear. We don't shrink from what we find inside. As we are open in our meeting with these dis-owned parts of our self, we also find transformation happening.

Awareness and understanding hold a warm quality of attention. In that warm attention, the things we have been afraid of are not so frightening, the parts of our self that we have judged as bad or wrong are not bad or wrong. They are simply lacking understanding. Like in any good adventure story, the challenges serve to reveal the resourcefulness of the hero. We discover our capacity for wise discrimination and an innocent awareness, the serpent and dove combination of Jesus' parables.

The turning point is learning to be with our self in ways where we come to experience the natural goodness that is within us. Through exploring the psychological self and the aware state of being, we come to rest in the goodness of our Being. This is the core of The Friend.

When we are comfortable with the basic goodness of our self, trust naturally follows. While this relaxation is often hard earned, the goodness itself is totally natural. Our basic goodness is as natural as the sun in the sky. And, like the sun in the sky, it has survived everything that we, or anybody else, have thrown at it so far. It has come through all of our life, the ups and the downs, and still shines the same way it did on the first day.

The Zen Search: Seeking the Bull

In the Zen tradition, the search for the Bull is a classic 1,000 year old story of the search for the self. A man loses his bull and goes looking for it. He struggles through swamps and over rough terrain, and often has only faint tracks of the bull to guide him. One day he finally sees the bull in the distance. Some days later he catches up with the bull and there is an epic test of wills to see who is the master of who. With the whip of meditative awareness and the staff of discipline, the man tames his bull and rides him back home.

This story continues today to be a guide for what it is like to realize that something important in our self is missing, and the Zen notion of what it takes to bring it back again. The Bull represents our True Nature, that precious something that has gone lost. The seeker has to find it again and then tame it with the skills he has learned through meditation and discipline.

In *The Friend* the story brings a new telling for new times. Our story carries a new light. It becomes less of a Zen warrior's story and more a friend's tale. In this way it reflects another time, another way of turning the wheel of truth.

It goes like this:

A bull is kept in a small shed at night, and works the fields in the day. One day he breaks free and heads for his native home in the wild.

A man goes looking for his bull. He curses the bull for its stupidity and for inconveniencing him so. He vows to thrash his bull and keep him under closer surveillance in the future. He fights against the dense bushes and wades through water that leaves his clothes wet and soiled. He climbs the mountains near his home, and slowly realizes that the bull has gone farther than he thought. The man has to choose to follow the bull or return home for the evening, and seeing that he has already come so far, he gives up the comfort of home for one night in order to be ready to catch his bull the next day. That night he curls up to sleep on the ground, his empty belly rumbling and a promise in his heart that he will make the bull pay for all this trouble.

The next day takes him further afield. He realizes he is entering new country, places he has never seen before. He is tired and hungry. He is even angrier at his bull. Thoughts and flies buzz around his head. He walks in irritation. That evening he sleeps a field again. He realizes he has come too far to go back without his bull.

The following day he is higher still in the forest. The air is cooler and he is surprised to find that he enjoys the wisp of wind on his neck. It feels cool and fresh on this hot day. He stops for a drink and is surprised to see how much light reflects from the water, and how fresh and clean it tastes. He can follow the tracks of the bull more easily now, and finds that his body walks faster and lighter from not having eaten his usual food.

Another day goes by. He is tired now and very hungry. The anger that kept him going has faded. A strange kind of melancholy settles in. He is sad. He doesn't know for what, but he can feel it as a heavy shadow that comes over his heart. He misses his home, he misses his bull, he wonders if his family is missing him, he wonders what the neighbors will think of him going out chasing his bull. He feels so sad that his legs refuse to walk another step. He sits in a meadow. He looks around to a field of white and yellow flowers that dance in the wind around him. These are normal flowers, the kind that he often cut in his own fields, but today he sees their freshness and color in the bright sun as if he had never seen these flowers before. He looks to the edge of the clearing and sees the sturdy evergreen trees of the forest. They stand so *silent, so strong. He feels sad again. Everything here is so beautiful and in its home. It is so different from his farm below where he works with mud and stones and plants that he puts in the ground himself and pulls out for harvest. Even in his tired, sad, state, he sees the wild beauty, something that was rare in his village. It touches him.*

He doesn't know what he is missing, but he knows he is missing something. Something important. Something real. Something he had given up hope for a long time ago.

He puts his head in his arms and cries. He cries for the wild beauty he sees, he cries for the man who lives far away from it, he cries for his tired body, he cries for missing his bull...and in the end he cries for no reason at all. It seems that the meadow grasses pull the tears from him. They are heard by the gentle forest winds.

He feels utterly, hopelessly lost. He promises that the next day he will turn around and walk home, if he could even find where home was again.

Then, he hears something indistinct. Behind him. He doesn't bother to look. It won't help anyway. He hears it again, and recognizes a familiar snorting sound.

He opens his eyes.

His bull. Standing in the clearing, just behind him.

He feels so much joy that he forgets his anger and all his promises. He jumps up and greets the bull as only old Friends can greet each other. He almost dances in delight, and then, feeling foolish in front of his bull, he catches hold of himself again.

He picks up his herding stick and starts to order the bull back to his stable. The bull backs away. He almost cracks the stick down and shouts, but this time he can't. He drops the stick and puts out his hand. He waits.

The bull eyes him carefully.

The man waits longer with his hand open.

The bull takes a half step forward, and then backs off again.

The man says, "Dear bull, please come with me. I am your master; I own you and employ you. I feed you. I built your shelter. You must come with me."

The bull backs away again.

The man feels sadness deep in his chest. "Dear bull, I have not been honest with you. Here, in your forest, I am not your master. You don't need my food. But I miss you. You are precious to me. I ask you to come with me.

"You are stronger than me; you are wiser than me in the ways of the woods. I don't know if I can find my way home without you. I don't know if I am strong enough to walk the whole journey back without you. Please, come."

The bull eyes him watchfully.

He shakes his open hand to show the bull its emptiness. He is surprised now by the feel of his hand; the asking has become an inviting. "Dear Bull," he says. "I ask you to come with me. I thank you for the lessons of the forest you have taught me in these days. I thank you for taking me into the wild lands of your home. I realize I have kept you in too small a stable at home. I realize you are a beautiful, wild creature and that I have turned you into a useful servant. I thank you for this lesson of the forest. I see that I have done the same thing to myself also. I have also turned myself into a plower of the fields and a merchant of the grains.

"Dear Bull, I also see that you have been my companion, my friend. I have beaten you and cursed you and ordered you around. Some day I was planning to eat you also. I apologize for my lack of respect. I can only tell you that what I have done to you, I have done to myself also. The harshness I put on you is a harshness that I have carried with myself. I promise that this day I will remember you as friend, companion, and that I will treat you with kindness and respect. Maybe you will even teach me to respect myself."

The bull comes forward and nuzzles his hand.

The man is surprised by the affection from the bull, and returns the affection with hand pats of his own. After all the days of walking, of being hungry, of drinking clear water, he can't believe how precious this meeting is. He puts his head on the bull's shoulder. For the first time in his life, he hears the bull's heartbeat. It is deep, strong, and steady. He feels grateful to the bull, and grateful to his own legs that brought him to this meeting.

He feels the bull shift its weight, and he steps back. The bull has come down into a kneeling position. He has never seen that before. He is utterly surprised. The bull turns its eye to him, and he sees what he thinks is an invitation. He steps forward and climbs on the bull's back. The bull stands up and carries him easily.

The man senses the strength and grace of the bull under him. He leans forward to the bull's ear.

"Dear Bull. I don't know where we are now, but I believe you do. I don't know if we are to go further into the forest, or to go home. I am tired and hungry, so I ask that we go home, but if the way goes further, then I will ride with you further."

Here it is said, the bull swishes his tail. He snorts his nostrils and clears them. He smells for water, and finding the smell of water, he follows it to the rivulet that leads down to the stream that leads down to the river that passes by the village below. Following the water soon brings them to a path, and the Way Home.

Part Two

The Journey Within

Ice

It's a January day in the north of Sweden. Wrapped in goose down and wool, I lie on my back on the ice of the 40-kilometer lake that was formed some thousands of years ago by a meteorite crashing down in the forest. The snow is falling gently, some of it landing on my eyebrows and beard, other flakes dancing just away, and still others kissing the exposed skin of my face with cool, wet caresses from the grey sky.

Mystic twilight time: the reflected light from the snow and ice on the ground are brighter than the light from the sky.

I love to lay still and hear the ice cracking through the lake and look at the grey sky above. Rest in the crystal clear silence of the Swedish forests. With eyes wide open, I can look into the overcast skies and enjoy millions of snowflakes pouring down, all white and dancing their way to earth. Changing focus, I can see individuals, the ones falling closer and closer. Each comes with their own dance, their own style of coming down, being who they are. Some days it seems endless, the outpouring from the sky. There are millions and millions of snow flakes, all part of some great field that takes on an individual personality as it comes down to earth.

I open my mouth and a few snowflakes drift in. Cool. Fresh. Delicate and wet. I fall back into remembering being in a workshop a few days earlier. I was leading a group of people in exploring the interface of meditation and psychological growth.

During one of the open sharing sessions, a man had asked me, "If so many people are looking for Truth, why have so few found it?"

Good question. I was touched with it. He was clear, sincere. I sensed an opening in the man behind the question. For a time, I didn't know what to say. In some ways, the question was too big for me. I waited, and I listened to the silence of the winter snow falling outside.

I remember slowly turning my face to the window and looking out to the grey sky. Without understanding yet what I was saying, I said, "Take a look outside at the snow falling down."

He was surprised, as were I and everybody else in the room. In these workshops we are trained to look inside ourselves for answers, not to the windows. Still, he turned to look at the gentle snowfall. After a moment he said, "OK, I see it."

"Good," I heard myself say. "Can you see that each of those snowflakes is fresh and pure and straight from God?"

"Yes," he said.

"How many of them are falling this very minute?" I asked.

"Millions, maybe more."

"Millions of little miracles in this moment, and how many of those miracles do you receive?" I asked.

A long silence. "I get it," he said.

And he did.

I fell totally silent. The depth of his question, the answer falling from the grey skies; I was just in between the two. I knew that his question was also my question, and that his answer was also my answer, and that somehow both the question and the answer came from a place beyond us both.

I loved the moment. Sure, I have been a therapist for over thirty years and have been guided by enlightened people and been touched and trained by many highly skilled professionals. Even so, in that moment, all of my history had vanished. I was just in the day, with the question, and quiet enough to hear falling snow. His question was so real that it called for a corresponding reality to come from me. For that I didn't go to the teachings I had learned or the experience I had gathered. I met him in the open place and waited for something new to form. I loved it.

Back on the ice again. Another snowflake on my cheek now…and one on my eyelashes slowly melting. It runs down my face like a tear with no name on it.

I don't move; just feel the cool smattering of snowflakes on my face, the firm support of the snow and ice under my back, the steady rhythm of my breathing, the overall sense of being held in something much bigger than me. The silence is like crystal…so pure and so fertile. I instinctively fall into listening to the silence.

Being friends with the silence, I feel its invitation. I expand, and the silence carries me into a bigger space, as though my body is now a hundred kilometers big and as high as the sky goes deep. The silence is breathing me, whispering in my ear, telling me its secrets and offering me its rest. I disappear into the silence, as though we are all one body, one mind. Timeless time passes.

A snowflake on my nose. Back down in the body again. Cold again, wet inside my nose. Another snowflake on my lips. Messages from the silence. I am amazed. Feeling my ribs expand and fall with each breath. Feeling the heart both as big as the sky and as small and fragile as the frozen snowflakes clinging to my beard.

Walking back across the ice to my cottage. The light there is still on, small but steady in the heavy Swedish night. There is a reassuring puff of smoke coming out of the chimney. The house will still be warm, I think. Just saying the word warm, I feel the cold and stiffness in my legs and shoulders. I brush the snow off my jacket. Nobody else is around this time of night. I'm glad for it. Half of me is still out in the sky's silence, another part of me is here and cold and touched.

Why are so few of us genuinely peaceful and happy?

Why is it that we live in a universe of such silence, beauty, blessings, and yet most of the time we don't even see the snowflakes, much less taste them?

I feel like the question and the answering have bitten me and dragged me out of a comfortable place into an opening, something like falling through a safe, warm world into a deep black hole. A place where I am very alone. It is not the first time I'm going there.

I remember the day I walked out of graduate school with a Master's diploma in religious studies from Union Theological Seminary. I hadn't gotten past the school gates when I realized with absolute clarity, "Having spent the last 16 years of my life in school, I still don't really know anything. Sure, I can read and write and answer all the questions on the tests, but does that mean I really know anything?"

The answer came as a clear, resounding "No." I realized how empty I felt from so many years of book studies. This realization opened up a hole inside... a deep emptiness that left me searching and uncomfortable for quite some time.

Walking slowly in the darkness. Back to my roots: when I can become still and silent enough, the answer to a real question will come out of the silence itself. The same way it happened in the group room when I went quiet with the participant's question, and in that silence the snow itself gave an answer. I feel like I am walking a Zen Koan now.

Crunchy ice, warm boots. The Koan way brings you face to face with an absurd question, one that is impossible to figure out rationally. You have to meet its absurdity with your own totality, and wait for something to come. Trusting, waiting, being both absolutely helpless and recognizing that it is only to this helpless place that the deeper answers will come. Many fears dance around the edge of true helplessness. Some days these fears go all the way back being a baby crying for milk.

I make a living this way. Being with people in therapy[2] situations brings out the Koan quality ten times a day or more. If I am really going to meet someone, really going to be with someone, I have to open myself to them. That means getting past the professional helper in me and the wounded victim in them, and allowing a meeting to happen that isn't defined by our roles. Staying present with people means being with them breath-by-breath, and feeling down into the unfolding of this moment without going too far ahead for answers and comfort and solutions.

Snow and silence and ice and the sense of danger from falling out of the comfortable world: if I am to find an answer that is real, genuine, and satisfying, it has to come from my own experience. It doesn't have to be something that I like, or even want...the truthfulness of it and the truthfulness of the way it has arisen brings the satisfaction. Such an answer has to be something that I don't grab or remember or hold on to. It has to arise out of the intimacy with the moment in the same way a rock climber will find the next place to put his hand by being absolutely present and intimate with the rock wall he is climbing. Too much information gets in the way, cuts the intimacy between my feet and the ice. Too much information becomes tension as I try to hold it, try to offer it.

The silence of the night fills me. The cabin's faint light is still a faint promise. My feet find their way even when it is too dark to see. I am out of the lake's ice and snow now, and am walking through a snowdrift of thick, crunchy snow. It is hard work to pick the way through knee-deep snow. Heavy breathing sounds contrast with the stillness of the night. "Sounds like a polar bear on the prowl," I think.

In the walking, questions and answers and questioning itself fade away. I am here. I am in touch. I am being guided, even if I don't know how and by whom and to where. It is happening.

The cold night air becomes almost warm. It holds me with a tenderness that I would not have expected. The crunchy snow is playful around my boots. Out of the heavy snow, suddenly the walking is easy. The door to the cabin is not far away.

Later, inside, with a warm cup of tea. Still full from the night. I sit by the fire. Relaxed, happy to see the warm orange flames. The flames bring comfort into my bones. Again I go back to the seminar room, and the question, "Why do so few people find the Truth that we are looking for?"

It has taken me now; I am totally with it. I remember the feeling of sitting in the leader's chair: alone, a sense of expectation surrounding me, the comfort of my own breath coming between my ribs. Somehow I was touched. This question cut to the core of all the group work we were doing. I let it in, like a stranger knocking at the door, and I had opened the door without really knowing what was to come next. I sensed the danger of the situation. I was no longer using my good brain for an answer, I wasn't really in control. I gave myself over to the not knowing and the silence, and the gap that they opened. It was hardly no time, but it felt to be a long time inside. I wondered what was going to happen—if anything—or if I was just going to sit there and appear dumb in front of a lot of people who had paid a lot of money to be with me. I had to let it happen now on its own, I was already in the gap where I didn't have any real fixed ground inside me for responding. Then, without any movement on my part, the snow and silence answered back through me.

The silence had said, "It is here. It is now. Can you drink of what is being offered here and now? Can you take the fullness of what is being offered and allow it into the tenderness of your heart?"

The answer was no-answer. It was Answering: inviting me to go through the senses into an open field of Presence. There in the open field of Presence the silence and the question and the answering and the open heart all came into one crystal clear moment of reunion. It was still vibrating in me. Answering doesn't fill the hole of the question. It leaves it wide open and says, "If you come into this open space then you will know what you are looking for."

A warm ember in the fire still glows. I stir the other logs to come back to the flame. My tea, half drunk, is gone cold. Somewhere I lost the time. I hear a logging truck come thundering by the house. It shakes the windows of the wood framed house and rattles dishes in the cupboard with its fierce intensity as it pounds over the frozen corrugated dirt road. I know the trucks only come this fast when it is very late and they have reasonable certainty that nobody else will be out on the road.

My body stretches and yawns. Now only my teeth to brush before bedding down for the night.

Lazy and warm in bed, I don't fall asleep immediately. Something too full is happening inside. I feel too rich. At the same time, I know it is all slipping away and that soon I will be totally asleep to the dark night and icy lake and big trucks.

In the morning the lake will be different in the pale northern daylight. There will be skaters and shouts and big cracks in the ice coming from the shifting temperatures. The silence will retreat to the deep woods, where it will hunker down with the moose and the lynx and wait its time through the snowmobiles and daylight until the full dark settles down again. In the daylight it is a different world, both for the lake and for me. In the morning's light I have to be practical with making plans for the coming year and writing a lecture presentation for the spring.

I come back to my breathing. Mostly breathing out now. Letting the day and the person who filled that day slip away. I fall into half awake, half asleep rest. Another truck rattles the windows and plates, but my body hardly moves this time.

No matter how full our lives are, no matter how much we know, no matter how good we try to be, there is always something missing. Some gap. Something profound.

And it is always disturbing when it knocks at the door. I work hard to build up skill and knowledge, to put money in the bank, to gather information and develop experience. I seek love and knowing and the sureness of the chair under my butt and the bed under my back.

And then. And then. And then comes another set of experiences, a newness that has to be responded to as a newness, and in that responding an awareness that I have to allow a way for the newness in me to meet the newness of the situation. It's like I am standing with both arms full of logs and seeing that there is already a fire and the fire is burning just fine without my logs. Often I make an inner protest, "But I have spent so long gathering all these logs and they have been heavy to carry through the deep snow…" but already I am putting the logs down so that my arms and hands and heart can be open.

I call it Space. The place between. The place we go where we are not hard and known and separate, but are quiet and soft and sensing and in touch. Knowledge and information are formed things. Space is the un-formed. Knowledge and information are things that we can remember. Space isn't. Space is like waking up early in the morning and finding a fresh snow has fallen and the path through the forest has to be found again.

Space is open and quiet. Non-aggressive. Infinitely full and empty at the same time. Now, after these years, we can be friends. Most of the time, anyway. I can enjoy her. I've found that she is not so easy to fool, and in the times when I'm wanting to fool myself, Space can be cold, hard, even harsh. Sometimes I want a piece of security that has my name on it and know that it sits there for me and me alone always and always. Then I run from Space. See her as angry Kali dancing on the ashes of my dreams. When I give up running and avoiding and wishing and trying not to be known, just as I am, then she comes back to me. She brings a familiar sense of Danger. The danger of losing control, risking to be made a fool by contact with something vast, something from beyond. After the danger signals warm down into glowing coals, I know that she will take my heart and whisper into it whatever I need to hear. Moment to moment. She takes everything I have away, and in return gives me what I need for this moment now.

I was asked, "Why is it so many people are looking for Truth and so few people find it?" Funny question. I see Truth show up in my office 50 times a day. I feel it in the group room for hours at a stretch. Truth is not such a hidden esoteric quality, something that you find during the full moon nights in the Great Pyramid. Truth is so ordinary that we look right past it. Maybe we don't find Truth because we don't really know what we are looking for. Maybe we think it is a solid thing, something we can have and know and keep in our left pocket and pull it out when we want. Probably the simple, shocking fact is that we don't really want it at all.

I smile.

In the comfort of the late night quiet I feel the dance of Truth going on inside me. Truth is always here. The problem is not with Truth, it is with us. Truth is here, but most of the time we aren't. Or, more accurately, the part of us that relates to truth isn't here. The part of us that knows Truth is Presence. Presence is the awake, aware part of True Nature. Presence talks to Space and Truth on a first name basis. Presence is the way we sense into truth, and feel it responding to us.

Space talks to us when we are willing to be intimate with Her. The way to be intimate with her is through presence, and the way to presence is to give up the known and open again into not-knowing.

Next morning. Sunrise at nine in the Swedish wintertime. The lake glistens from the light of the low in the sky sun reflected off the snow and ice. I sit in my morning chair to enjoy the awakening of the day with a cup of jasmine tea. The fire crackles beside me. The dinosaur trucks are in hiding for another night, and the frozen road carries the occasional commuter in his gray Volvo.

Another smile. Something deep and familiar is moving inside.

We don't know Truth because we have lost contact with the part of us that senses Truth. Presence senses Truth. The personality that most of us live in doesn't.[3]

So this is what He meant. The Buddha Himself. He had said the root cause of suffering is ignorance. I hadn't understood that for thirty years. In my world, the people who lived in the shacks on the farms were called ignorant.

In the morning light, the face of ignorance is suddenly clear. It has nothing to do with education. Ignorance means we don't know Truth because we don't know our selves.

I sit up in the chair. I feel challenged. We aren't with Truth because we aren't with ourselves. All day long there is a discomfort, a pushing away from the simple experiences of our self. We push away almost immediately—a rejection here, a spacing out there, a sense of only being partly here, a hope that we can wish for something different...We cut off from the here and now part of our selves in the longing for something different, something better. We don't have a friendly, open contact with our selves. We are frightened to have real contact with others. These are the faces of ignorance.

Ignorance is not a noun; it is a verb. It is not something that did or didn't happen. It is an activity that we engage it. We do it. Relentlessly. Seen heartfully, ignorance is a state of the art filtering system that works 24 hours a day, 7 days a week.

Grasping and seeking: the active forms of ignorance. I push away from what is, and I try to hold on to what I want. Sounds silly, like a kid's game, something that I could just smile at if I saw it in my sister's kids. But I'm not a kid now; I'm caught in this system. I push and pull on myself all day long. I'm in a kid's game with myself, and I don't know how I got there and I don't know how I get out of it. The one thing I do know is that being caught in this system is very uncomfortable. And, fighting against it only makes it worse. Like struggling in quicksand or wrestling with a spider's web.

I want to know more: How does this come? What gives it its power? What makes us cling to such a system when it is clearly dysfunctional for bringing us fulfillment?

My meditation master Osho says it in a different way than Buddha. He doesn't use the word "ignorance" very often. What he repeatedly says is "You don't know who you are."

A strange thought: "I don't know who I am." How in the world could that possibly be true? How can I live with someone for a whole lifetime and not know who he is?

In the beginning of working in Osho's field, I participated in a workshop where we were asked fifty times a day "Tell me who you are."

From 5.30 in the morning until 10pm we were either asking

the question or listening to someone else grapple with it. After the first three hours, we were already in trouble. We realized that we consider our labels to be ourselves, but in the light of the questioning, our nametags fell off. Our names aren't who we are. Our jobs aren't who we are. Our gender isn't who we are. Our family is not who we are. There were many things giving vague hints at who we are, but nothing really hitting the nail on the head. Even more disconcerting was the awareness that I had been living as though I knew who I was, but I didn't really know at all. It was like I am driving my car at high speed without really knowing where the road goes and why I am even driving it. I get some confirmation seeing other people also driving their cars so fast on the same road...and then the dawning desolation that says, "They don't know either."

Sooner or later the "who am I" workshop brought all of us into the same kind of shock the early quantum physicists must have felt when they discovered that inside all the hard and solid things of our daily reality is a world of space and energy and probability where we don't know at all what is really going on. The appearance of reality—firm, reliable, existing in time, having very clear, fixed borders—is only an appearance. The fact of reality is space, no-time, energy, probability (not reliability), and constant movement that is somehow both scientifically foreign and subjectively related to the consciousness that views it. The same thing is true inside us. We carry fixed assumptions about who we are, but in reality these assumptions are only external representations. The real fact of who we are is like a field, a field of consciousness which doesn't easily fit into names, identity badges, and history.

I underwent the "Who am I" workshop and then helped to lead another twenty or thirty of them. Nobody really knew who they were. Sometimes in the flash of brilliance or exhaustion, would come a sudden Zen-like awakening: I am just what is here in this moment... I am the soft unfolding of my hand, and the tenderness of my exhalation: little jewels of awakening coming out of days and nights of dark, hard work.

Time switch: again I'm back in the cabin in the Swedish pale light.

How is it that we don't know who we are?

Can this be just an accident? Or is it intentional?

I am excited. So here it is again. The question: "Why is it that so many of us don't find what we are looking for?" starts unfolding.

Why? Better yet, How? How does this happen? What are the mechanics of it? What is the logic of the machinery that we are caught in?

A cold realization follows the wind and its low lying clouds outside. Buddha designed a system to work with ignorance 2500 years ago, and yet there is probably more ignorance going on today than in his time. Other great teachers have tackled the same themes and also met with limited success. Who am I to get involved here?

I recognize a sense of danger inside. Asking a Real question is going to line me up with a Real answer and that Real answer is probably going to be like sharing a small iceberg with a large Polar Bear. It's going to shake me up. Meeting a real question takes me on a journey. A personal Odyssey where I will be tested and challenged and through those tests and challenges let go of old, sometimes dear things, and discover something new. Not only discovering a new land out there, but also discovering some hidden parts of myself. The kind of resources inside that Odysseus found on his journey or that a rock climber will find when he takes on a tough climb. I might win, I might lose…either way I have to let go and play.

Am I ready for it?

The danger signal again. We know each other well. If I can open to the danger in the same way I lie on the ice and look at snow, then the danger signal will talk to me and take me along.

Already the process has started. Now to relate with it. If I can meet danger in trust and presence, it will shake my body and touch my heart and then, sooner or later, whisper in my ear. Danger will take me in its cave and tell me of things unknown to people who avoid danger. If I meet danger with courage, it will take me to places where my question converts into its answer.

I pull on my overalls and snow boots. First to go out for the sun and crisp air and the joy of kick sledding over the ice. I knew that the intention was set. I had a date with my danger signal. I didn't have to wait around for it; it would find me when I was ready.

Sometime later, after the sled was parked away and the fire re-kindled and my tired legs stretched out from the rocking chair, the shakiness comes back. I know better than to try to avoid it this time. It isn't so pleasant to be with, but I don't really have a choice. The beginning of things is always hard for me anyway. I stand up. I let the shaking come up my legs, into my belly and chest. Slowly my breathing rises to a tempo where it and the shaking are at the same speed. I stay curious about the location of the shaking in my body…heart, legs, belly…or places even deeper inside. When I feel the location, I bring my breath to the place and allow the breathing and the shaking to merge into a single movement, like the way a rider melts down and becomes one with a galloping horse. More danger signals, then a relaxing as the horse trusts that the rider is really with him. I ease into a deeper level of connection. I ask to be taken to the place where the shaking comes from.

I let the experience take me along and it falls into different layers. First comes the body shaking and a vague sense of danger. Then there are layers of emotion also activating into fear, grief, longing…the usual suspects, old friends by now. The breathing carries me through these introductory layers, and then clears through the zone where they live and takes me into an inner landscape, further inside. Quieter now, more open, not really sure of my shape or age any more. Less fear, more a sense of wonder. My bull has bolted through the woods and is now walking on a high slope, far above the tree line. The air is crisp and cool as the wind plays on my face. I can see forever.

The question returns: what is it that keeps us from being happy?

I feel a pull to this question, like I will be meeting it for the first time, again.

I wait with it. I get the image of a Buddhist monk, his bowl in hand, going for his daily begging. This time I am holding the bowl in my own hands, asking for what my own being will give me for this night's question. Waiting and appreciating whatever is offered.

The breathing slows down and I am dropping deeper inside myself. Something has responded to the patience of my approach. Buddha's begging bowl of non-aggression is doing its work, again.

Looking back at where I have been, I see that the first answer to my question has already come. One reason we are not happy is that we don't have an easy time making real contact with our self. We are constantly reacting against our self. The begging bowl stands for acceptance...and it is only through the helpless acceptance that the mind quiets and allows me to enter more deeply.

Acceptance brings intimacy. I am feeling touched. It is like I have taken off a big overcoat, and now can feel the weather on my skin. There are sensations of pleasure and discomfort, both at the same time. I allow my breath to quicken and carry me into this place of feeling.

At first I feel wide, expansive. Deliciously free. A tingle of ecstasy touches me like cold mountain air on my skin and I am delighted. Then follows more relaxation, and merging into timelessness.

After a while comes a buzzing sensation. The situation is

turning from open awareness and heading into a pain place. The bright open place of feeling starts to turn dark as a sense of compression sets in. My breathing quickens again to the intensity. I remember other experiences I have had with pain. In those experiences I have learned that trying to get out only makes it worse. The only thing to do is dive for the bottom; head for the heart of the pain and meet it.

I feel the darkness around me. A sense of desolation and loneliness. No escape and no light. Then comes a flash of awareness, a remembrance. It starts with a little appreciation: no wonder the danger signal was so strong. This dark, painful place is pretty rough. Darkness. Pain. Aloneness. I keep sensing. Then another discovery arises. I am still awake here. I am here. I remember to turn into the heart of the darkness: I ask, "What is the worst of this dark place? Is it the pain? Or the dark? Or the aloneness in pain and dark?" And the answer comes right away: "I can handle pain and darkness if I am not alone. The aloneness is the killer."

Something settles.

I know that the aloneness is the edge. It feels like complete, utter helplessness surrounded by a sense of abandonment, like I have been discarded or forgotten. I don't have any idea of how to cope with that, but at least I know what is pressuring me so intensely.

Suddenly, in this black internal space a small sphere of pearly white light spontaneously appears. I realize that I am not alone. What a surprise. I didn't expect any help here but something/someone is with me.

I ask this sphere, "Who are you? Where do you come from?" There is no answer, just a slight play in the way it moves. I wonder, "Is this from me? From my meditation master? From some other person?"

I don't know, but what I do know is that the feeling of being alone is gone. Somehow there is a supporting presence with me even in this place of pain. There is a light in my dark: I am not abandoned and forgotten.

I am left in this big, dark, open space with my little white light friend. I feel peace and comfort. Deep rest. Again a sense of timelessness.

After some time, my eyes open. I see the fireplace, the kitchen sink, and the dishes on the rack. There are so many things around me. Hard, solid things, but strangely related, like we are all part of the same family. I hear the fire still softly crackling and I become aware of its warmth even now. I'm in the outer, normal world again, but this time with a sense of family in it.

The memory of my question returns. "Why is it that so few of us find what we are looking for?" Another layer of the answer falls in place. In the last hour and a half I have been below the level of mind that is constantly thinking. Below the thinking mind is the pain body,[4] the place where our emotional memories swim like the mythic sea monsters of the ancient oceans. Navigating the pain body is very difficult unless you know its ways. In the pain body experience is very raw. If we protect against the pain, we end up fighting for our lives or being thrown out and back in the world of thoughts again. If we don't protect against the pain, there is every sense of being overwhelmed, taken over by something so awful that we promised our selves we would never let it happen again. It is like drowning.

I wait. The realization I am not alone sinks in deeper. There is a sense of tenderness inside. The pain experience has brought a new sense of intimacy with myself. I feel my body sitting peacefully warm again.

Negotiating the pain body brings realness and rest.

The luminous friend who came to me this time was a stranger. I still wonder who sent him or where he came from. His Presence gave me a key, a reminder of non-aloneness, and in that support field, my own intelligence could travel down and through the Pain body.

Clearly the way out is down and in, not up and out.

The danger signal was not for nothing...I was being taken on a journey again. A new set of islands and seas for Odysseus.

Why is it so few of us find what we are looking for? Another answer to this question takes its place. Inside us is a lot of unresolved old pain. While it is hard to let go of surface mind that is thinking; it can be terrifying to be in the pain world underneath. The pain body kicks up too many memories from childhood, kicks up too many ghosts. When we get too far lost in it, we become like a child again and experience it from the insecure place of a child. We can't avoid encountering it like a lost child, and we can't get through it this way either.

Tonight breathing was my way. Breathing and turning my awareness to the darkest part of the pain. Not avoiding.

And what happens then? What happens when we fall down through the black hole of the pain body? We go into emotional pain and then into an existential pain of aloneness and then, it feels like we get sucked into something like a black hole in space and released out on the other side. For me it has usually brought a new light on the other side. Tonight it is rest; I'm in a gentle pain-free body holding a grateful heart and a quiet and clear mind. A rack of dishes that brings a smile to my face and a small, dancing fire that gives me more than I ever asked for.

I feel a sense of grace and the return to simplicity that comes with grace. The relentless march of time has turned into a solo flute playing to eternity.

Later...the end of the night. I sit by the small fire in wonder.

I feel utterly quiet.

A breath of gratitude comes and goes and the fire crackles on while a solo candle flickers in the window. No more trucks will be coming now, and it is too early for the skaters. The night is so late that it is almost morning, the time just in between one state and another.

The journey of the question has taken me through the dark

night and back into the grey light of early dawn. Here is the Grey world, the place between dark and light, the place where I find a sense of beginnings.

As my eyes adjust to the light, I see more clearly what the grey light has to offer. When I am outside myself, I see the world and relate to things from that place. Life can be good, a lot seems to happen, but for the most part I don't really get it. Outside myself I am not so real, and not being so real I can handle only small doses of reality coming my way. On the same day I see so many different things and have so many different feelings that even I wonder who I am. Coming inside myself is not easy, but each step inwards feels more true. In this more true feeling there is a deep sense of joy, but to live in this more true place is not very easy either. I am aware of fear and hate and separation and anger and control and how I impose those qualities on the people and things around me. Often when I am more true and inside myself, I am not such a nice guy. I like being more true, but I carry a lot of regret for how my inner dinosaur can stomp his way through the garden.

Coming through the pain body brings me into a new sense of self, a fresh sense of realness and contented Presence. There is a warm relaxed love in my heart. This warm relaxed love seems to come up into my eyes, and what I see is also imbued with a sense of love and friendliness. The same thing that is in me I can see in most everybody else. The light in my heart makes Ikea's dishes glow as objects of wonder. The squeak of the rocking chair on the wooden floor has overtones of humor and delight.

Back to my question. The grey light says, "It's all in the awareness. The way that is hidden for one set of eyes is wide and open for another. One set of eyes sees confusion and darkness and pain and competition, and the very same eyes can see love and fulfillment and grace. It all depends on who is looking, on what layer of our being is allowed to look."

I know it. The grey light at the end of the night brings it all to me.

The same self that separates me from my self, the same self that gives me so many problems with so many other people…in the grey light of dawn this self glows with Presence. In the warmth of the moment, this same self is now the way home, even now it carries the seeds of Reunion.

Water

There was a man named Mojud who worked as an inspector of weights and measures in a small village. Getting on in age, he was looking forward to his retirement and pension in only a few more years. In the mean time, every day after work he made a practice of taking a walk by the River.

One day, in his customary walk, he saw something of an apparition appearing before him. A bright smiling man in shimmering green came walking towards him. He looked like a king or a visiting God from outer space. His name was Kidhr.

When they met, Kidhr addressed Mojud: "O man of bright prospects."

Mojud looked around to see whom he was talking to. Here was a king in shimmering green talking to a lifelong government employee. "Man of bright prospects?" Looking forward to a retirement didn't seem to be the brightest of prospects, even to Mojud.

Mojud more or less said, "Huh?"

Kidhr wasn't easily put off. He said, "If you want to know your bright prospects, then meet me here at the River tomorrow." Kidhr then vanished.

Mojud was in turmoil for the night. A lot of "Yes...but" went through his mind and he was distracted the next day at work. "Do I or don't I?" racked his mind and heart.

Somehow, there he was again by the River that afternoon, and, true to his promise, so was Kidhr.

Kidhr wasted no time: "O man of bright prospects! If you want to know the way, take of your clothes and throw yourself in the river... perhaps someone will save you."

Mojud was surprised, shocked even, but in the glow of the man's Presence, he did so. He undressed and jumped into the river.

Sometime later, floating downstream, Mojud encountered a fisherman in his boat. The fisher man said, "Crazy man, how did you come to be in the River? Who are you and where are you going?"

Mojud said, "My name is Mojud. I don't know where I am going."

The fisherman shook his head and reached out his hand. He took him in his boat and said, "Come stay with me for a while. You can help me here in my work by the River."

And so began the story of one of the greatest teachers in Sufism...[5]

By the river, the day starts early in India. Even as the orange sun rises through a smoky sky, you can hear the slapping sounds of wet clothes hitting the rocks. These are the hand-wash dhobis doing the community laundry. Some dhobis work quietly, intent on their mission while others call to each other and sing the morning's stories from the households where they work. Sooner or later the sound of laughter joins in the day's grunts.

I rise every morning before the sun and make a cup of tea and sit on the little balcony overlooking the river. Eyes open, I see a play of colors in the rising of the day—the saris on the rocks, the white shirts being redeemed in the brown water, the orange turbans of the washer men, the shiny bangles on the women's arms. Eyes closed, I hear the river sounds. After a little while, the cries and gurgles and morning shouts bring me down to the river and invite me in. The sounds are around me, and then inside me... taking me into a river running through my inner space.

My meditation master Osho teaches that consciousness is like a river. It is an inner river that flows through all of us. He says that relaxing into the river allows us to go deeper and deeper into our own nature.

He also promises that every flowing river, sooner or later, reaches its home in the ocean.

He says that our identities, our sense of self, can be like rocks in the river. The "I" stands outside the flow of consciousness, trying to maintain itself and protect its self. The rock of "I" creates the illusion that we are a single, separate, real person, a known shape and quantity that we have created.

As therapists we know that inside the rock of "I" lives a host of emotions, attitudes, hurts. The castle of "I" looks like it protects a king, but usually it covers a beggar. The rock-like protection systems of our "I" don't allow the river to flow in its natural course. Where the water meets the rocks, there is a field of disturbance. The water retreats from this disturbance and flows where the way is open and clear.

Psychology of the Buddhas

Our job as therapists in Osho's Commune in India in the 1970's was to bring attention to the inner rocks: to clear the protections and reveal the fears, the angers, the hidden sadness, the inarticulate voices of the child. To recognize the disturbance fields that they create in the river of consciousness. We were encouraged to explore beyond the narrow limits of old identity, to see what happens when these rocks are cracked, or melted, and integrated. By releasing feelings, we could release the beliefs that bound us into past identity. In this way we could open into genuine meditation and allow the inner river to flow deeply, quietly, true to its own nature.

For those of us who came to India from the west, Osho's insight opened a new field, the bridging of psychological growth from the Western world and traditional meditation from the East. In the west we were trained to work with the rocks… in fact we thought we were the rocks! We knew ourselves as solid identities made up of ideas and emotions, and wanted to be better people by improving the rough parts of our identity.

In the East, the land of meditation, the emphasis was on the river. Indians gathered to be near a master and join in the flow of his consciousness. The rocks were immaterial; they just were temporary impediments to a flow of consciousness that would always find its way around them.

Osho gave us the vision of meditation and identity being two parts of one field of consciousness. It was time to merge Eastern psychology and Western psychology into the "Psychology of the Buddhas." Traditional Western psychology was based on the experience of personality and ego. It had a lot of insight into the way personality develops, but western psychology didn't include the deeper states of Being that one finds through meditation. On the other hand, Buddhist psychology offered precise, clear descriptions of the transcendental self and the obscurations of ego activity that separate us from knowing this transcendental self. However traditional Buddhism was missing a certain kind of dynamism that comes from embracing personal experience—illusion and all. Buddhism was also ensconced in some heavy cultural baggage where the form of the culture created a heavy overlay on the emptiness Buddhism sought.[6]

Bringing them together created the opportunity for a new way of being to emerge: a vibrant Buddhism without the baggage, and a psychology truly based on experiences of Being. For this new way that Osho coined the expression "Zorba the Buddha."

This combination was quite new to a New York trained therapist. Like fusion music, fusion therapy had never really happened before. This new kind of therapy was as unique as Jan Gabarek's sax solo sitting on top of Hari Prasad's flutes and Zakir Hussain's tabla riffs: a delightfully improbable combination.

The essence of Western therapy is to identify with thoughts and emotions and work through them. For us Westerners, nothing happens until we get real and own our anger and fears and such. In therapy it doesn't work to talk about anger or fear. The real stuff comes when we say "I *am* angry" or "I *am* afraid" with no holding back. The more totally we jump into our feelings, the more totally we can process them.

Further, a big part of a therapy process is finding the roots of our present emotions in the experiences of our past. We look at our present feelings as extensions of past experiences, especially the experiences of early childhood. We gain understanding and compassion by linking our present reactions with the stresses we faced when we were in our formative early years. From this place we can discharge old emotion, understand where it came from, and be more real in daily life.

In contrast, the essence of meditation is to not identify with thoughts or emotions. The basic teaching in meditation is to simply watch these things without getting engaged in them. Instead of saying, "I am angry," a meditator is likely to report, "Anger is in my system, but it is not me."

Also, meditators are encouraged to drop the past and just be here. This means to dis-identify with the history of the mind, to not buy into all the mental and emotional baggage that we carry. Instead of helping us be better people, meditation's aim is to realize "No-self", the understanding that we aren't any of the identities that we entertain in our psyche. We are actually the being that is beyond thoughts and feelings.

You can appreciate that bringing meditation and therapy together appears impossible. Theoretically, meditation and therapy don't belong in the same room. This play of opposites and impossibilities was just the kind of living koan that Osho loved to create.

Rivering

Nearly everyone who came to the Osho Commune was touched by the depth and clarity of Osho's presence. He offered a living reality of love and timelessness that many of us had read about, but had never actually met.

In the light of his presence, we realized how frozen we were.

We were caught in trying to be somebody good, somebody right. We weren't connected with our heart or with our deepest being. We were up on the surface of the self and trying desperately to make that surface self look good.

We had no idea what the nature of our heart was really like or if our being truly was flowing like a river. And the only way to really find out was to get wet.

From our own experience in Western personal growth therapies, we knew that we had a busy mind and an armored body that was full of tensions. These tensions were related to many of the emotional conflicts that we carried inside, the fears and angers and grieving that we had learned to suppress.

In this state it is not realistic to think that one could simply sit still in meditation and find deep and permanent bliss. That was asking too much. In fact, it was too much to expect that we would meet anything more than a lot of thinking and uncomfortable feeling.

To go inside to our natural hearts and being, first we need to discharge the accumulated toxic energy of our body-mind, and jump back into the river of our emotions. Maybe this river of emotions would take us further into personal pain and separation; maybe we would find out that we really are a bad kind of person. Maybe getting into our feelings would take us away from being cool, silent spiritual types and into being libidinous ego monsters...the very opposite of the spiritual ideal that attracted us. It was a huge gamble.

Osho designed cathartic meditations and a series of therapies to push us further into the river. Soon everything that you could find in California or in New York was also in Poona. Encounter, massage, Rolfing, Bio-energetics, Creativity, Alexander Technique, Breath therapies, Reichian bodywork: the whole lot. Even so, it had a twist. In the west we did work on our selves to be better people, for self improvement. In Poona that notion of self-improvement went out the window. Instead of self improvement, the basic theme was self revelation; that is to be honest and open with what was truly inside...to acknowledge the self that we really were and drop the mask of the self that we are trained to be.

This can be very frightening stuff. We had come together to be strong, spiritual, silent, loving people and in an hour's group session we were literally at each other's throats. Many times we were in murky water as the repressed self came out in full force. Old pain, hate, attitudes, sexuality...you name it. The whole lot was provoked; anything was fair game to stretch us out of the self that we had learned to be and to fall into the self that we actually were. This was often scary, humiliating, bewildering, and overwhelming. At the same time, there was exhilaration and freedom and love and tenderness as the ego crusts dropped off and the river of being began freely flowing.

As therapists we were in such a world for 350 days a year. In the day in and day out grind of combining Osho's presence with intense therapy experiences, a few signature points came through.

The first is surrender. The key to being in water is surrender. Water is about learning to flow. When we fight the flow inside or around us, then the water can't take us on its journey.

To be at home in the feeling world, we quit resisting it. Like Mojud in the Sufi story, we get naked and wet. Over the hundreds of breath therapy sessions and bio-enegetic sessions I led, I saw that most of us live out of touch with our deeper feelings. We carry on as if they are simply not there. When provoked — as happens in bio-energetic therapy or encounter groups or the like – we still don't get immediately into our deeper feelings. We go into a fuzzy zone where we meet the resistance to our feeling. We meet the part of us that denies the feeling. We still try to stay in civilized control against what is instinctual and hot inside. We resist feeling angry, and when anger arises, we feel our resistance to it but not really the white hot experience of the anger itself.

We do this with every strong emotion. We don't feel the actual emotion, rather we feel our <u>resistance</u> to the emotion. An emotion needs to be felt in order to transform it. If we only feel the resistance to our emotions, we never can release the real emotion.

Resisted anger can last for generations. Anger that is experienced in the body and breath will never last longer than five minutes. As this is true for anger, it is also true for all the big heavy emotions that we carry. I have never seen an emotion last longer than five minutes when it is genuinely felt.

Another key is trusting the river. When we are real and alive with our feelings we melt out of Ice-olation, and something deep inside us starts flowing again. That something that is flowing is highly intelligent. It knows where it is going, what it is seeking. Often through the door way of the dis-allowed feelings comes a renewed, profound sense of love. We discover that every feeling will flow towards love when we allow it.

The river of our being will naturally go towards love, like a river heading towards the ocean. We can float on that. We don't have to effort. The river of being carries us along with a sense of timeless grace. The deeper water carries both stillness and an intrinsic movement. Each moment is round and still in itself. At the same time, we feel the pull of the ocean.

Rocking
It is not by accident that the rocks of personal identity happen.

There are good reasons we prefer to "rock" (resist) rather than to flow in the river of our consciousness.

From our childhood training, we sense our own emotions as problematic, even dangerous. For example, anger is not allowed, and when it does surface, it makes for many dramatic, messy situations. Fear tends to isolate us, make us feel even more alone and also unworthy. Sadness is more acceptable, but it leaves us feeling without energy. Deep feeling usually brings us into aloneness. This kind of aloneness also carries judgment in it: we shouldn't be the way we are. As we grow up, we hear this so much from others that we adopt it for ourselves as well. "Don't be afraid, don't be angry…What is the matter with you? You look so sad. Don't be sad, cheer up!"

We carry the impression that our emotions are unacceptable and indicative of a poorly functioning personality (at best) or a chronic weakness of moral fiber (at worst).

In order to get control over our selves, we tend to close down the heart center in the chest and lock feeling in the stomach and belly. When we have locked down these lower centers, we can then experience less feeling and be more in our mental world, the mind. The mind is safer, more controllable, and more easily disguised.

So we learn to lock down our experience. We learn to control the emotions that naturally arise and substitute them with the mental states that we create. As we lose contact with our body and heart, we lose contact with the natural flow towards love that is inside us. Actually, we lose the whole reference of a healthy. natural self. We learn to live by rules and commandments (at least ten or more) and to fit the expectations others have of us.

This makes for rocks of identity. We instinctively want to protect our "I"dentities. To make them solid and real, to be someone we know and can count on. This "I" tends to harden into a fixed person that everyone can call by name. It tries to live forever in its rock-like form. The "I" is our protection, and we naturally want our protection to be secure and eternal.

As it is that this protection system is our own creation, it never feels totally secure. It is like riding a bicycle; if we don't keep feeding it with energy, it will slow down and we will fall over. In order to compensate for this inherent sense of insecurity, we continually add to the defenses and put our attention even further out to the protection systems. We feed the protection system with all our available resources and, over time, come to regard the health of the protection system the same thing as our own personal health.

Ignorance becomes our ally.

These rocks and rivers look like very different things—self and no-self, mind and no-mind. However, by taking them as a living koan, a new appreciation for the unity of these opposites comes.

First, here is a little more background into the roots of each system.

How the Self is Formed—the western version

According to recent psychological theory, our sense of self arises through contact with the outside world. When we see mother, we know our self as child. When we see sister, we know our self as brother. When we see teacher, we know our self as student...and so on. We learn who we are through our I-Thou[7] relating with objects and people around us. The experience of Thou is what tells us who the "I" is.

In between the "I" and the Thou is a state of feeling. This feeling quality (called "affect") determines the relationship. A strong feeling between the "I" and Thou forms a strong sense of identity in us. One could say that we create identities as reaction to strong feelings, that intense feeling generates an equally intense creation of identity. This is like the way an animal will freeze in response to imminent danger. In times of emotional stress, we simply freeze up, and in that freezing we lock a sense of self in place. Once that sense of self is locked in, then it becomes a reference point for us. The insecurity that formed into an "I" remains within us. It will always be seeking new forms of protection.

Good feelings have a smooth, broad quality that makes for a soft identity pattern. We flow with good feelings. There is no strong identity formed in that flowing. However, harsh feelings are sharp and painful. They create hard, fixed identity responses. These hard, fixed identities are contractions from the shock of being hurt. The sense of self we get from a mother's rejection or a teacher's anger is equal to the shock we feel from such things. Such hurts cut deeply into the open psyche of a child. The identity that forms in response will be significant and deep.

The identities formed in pain stand as guardians for us against future pain. From childhood on, we gather the identities that guide us for the rest of our life. Because the identity formed in pain is harder than the identities formed in love, we remember the wounds much longer than we remember the love.

In other words, we turn into rocks. We harden our selves so that we are protected. The bigger and stronger sense of self we can create, the more secure we feel.

How the self is formed—the eastern meditator's version
In the Western psychology, we learn who we are through relationships with the outside world. In meditation, we learn who we are through contact with our own consciousness, the awareness and experience we have in the present moment. In Buddhist psychology, no amount of information from the outside will ever give us knowledge of the Self. We might learn things about our self, but this is not the same as knowing the Self. Knowing the Self is to meet it and participate in its reality.

In the meditator's world, the self is forming every moment. Our self is not really a noun, it is a verb. It is a process in action. The process of self-ing unfolds to our consciousness, and depending on our attachments and aversions, we select what aspects of the self we make real. Things we hold on to or things that we push away become solidified by the nature of our engagement with them. What we make real by our mental actions becomes real to our experience.

In other words, we create our self through the play of our own mind. The moment to moment reactions of our mind tell us what is real and who we are. We are not made into a self, rather we are constantly making this self.

In the meditative tradition, the way into our inner world is a way of watching and not reacting. In this way we gradually learn to quit struggling with our experience. We learn to release the identities that are formed in our struggle with our experience. Over time we can taste the grace of each moment coming in a brand new package that has no outer reference of past and future.

The real art of meditation is being aware of our ego activities without reacting against them. How?

Buddha demonstrated this art by having a disciple sit next to a muddy pond. Buddha stirred the pond and then asked, "How is the water going to get clear again?" The disciple said, "Don't do anything more, and it will clear itself." Buddha then invited him to watch the pond settle into clarity and to use that as an example for settling of his own Mind.

Watch and wait! Awareness dissolves reactivity. It brings us into a relaxed surrender to our own experience.

This surrender releases consciousness back into its natural flow. It is in this natural flow that we discover something deeper than our created self.

Ego

The common ground for both the western and eastern traditions is that the normal sense of self is formed in reaction. This created self is called ego. In the western tradition, the ego is an identity (or collection of identities) that come in reaction to external sources. While in the eastern meditative tradition, the ego is a series of reactions to its own experiences. Both eastern and western approaches agree that the ego is a created entity.

From this agreement on the creation of the self, the paths diverge. In the west attention has gone to supporting the ego, to making the self strong and integrated. This approach basically recognizes the protective function of identity or ego. Since identity is created as protection against outside threats, then the stronger the better. In this tradition, flowering comes from a secure sense of self that projects its strength out into creative action in the world around.

In the Eastern meditative traditions, the confused mind is called ego. In this tradition, ego is something of a garbage bag. It is a consciousness which is so full of accumulated materials that it doesn't know its own reality. This self holds heaps of undigested, unassimilated psychological material. Our pre-occupation with our internal landfills is what keeps us from realizing our true, clear nature. From this point of view, the solution is to dissociate from the personal self, to recover the awareness that is separate from the personal self.

Both approaches have their beauties and their limits. Common to both is the recognition that as soon as we have an ego then we have problems. We come into a place of duality, of separation. If we follow the western tradition of making an Identity into the real self, then we are stuck with an artificially created entity. This created self fights with all our other identities; it is a poor substitute for the full range of who we are. Ego will keep us oriented to present living from the place of past experience. It will generate ignorance of what is here and now in order to maintain its references to the past. Even more fundamental, affir-mation of ego as self means that we substitute created identities for the reality of True Nature. This substitution of the remem-bered self for the True Self leads to feeling deficient no matter how successful it is in projecting wonderful things into the environment.

If we follow the eastern path we recognize that being inside an ego brings duality. The more we live from a place of duality, the more separate we become. Through the practice of non-attachment, we quit feeding this artificial self with our attention and energy. However, in this approach we can easily dissociate from personal experience. We don't value the play of feelings and mind inside us, and in that meditative denial of the personal self leads to a sense of ego as enemy.

Zorba the Buddha

Zorba the Buddha is a way beyond the limitations in the two styles. From the west, we can understand ego by opening to the feeling quality that ego tries to protect. That means releasing into the feeling states that operate behind our ego positions. When we do, we realize the ego system is our defense system. It knows how to defend against attacks. It is built to keep us safe from pain and attacks. It will fight tooth and claw to protect us, and it will fight tooth and claw to protect us even from our own intrusions.

When we make ego the enemy, we set up an adversarial relationship with our own defense system. When we fight with our own ego, it senses danger and aggression coming against it. It reacts by contracting, protecting, and multiple other strategies to confuse the invader. The water of consciousness gets very muddy here as we struggle against our selves. In the struggle with our own defenses, ego usually wins.

Opening our heart to the feeling quality inside us, and exploring the feeling states with a curious mind quickly brings depth. In that depth is a sense of relaxed humanness, a sense of being at home with the self and knowing that this self is fundamentally good, no matter how it is perceived in its external manifestations.

From the Buddhist tradition we understand that ego is not a fixed thing. It doesn't really exist as a solid entity. It never has been solid and never will be. It really is activity, the motion of our mind working on itself. The relentless high speed activity of the mind creates the appearance of a substantial object, but this appearance is illusory. Questioning the activity and slowing it down will reveal the fundamental openness of the whole system.

When we realize that we are not identities, then we can quit trying to improve our identities. We let go of the effort to be better persons. When we quit trying to improve ourselves, the door opens for discovering the beauty and precision of what we already are, our inner nature. Being real becomes more important than being perfect. Being true to our nature becomes the quest of daily living.

Melting

When it is warm, ice melts into water. Sometimes this happens quickly, sometimes it takes eons. Either way, living evolution brings hard, formed things (like us) back into a fluid state.

This warmth comes from two main sources. The first is friction: times of stress. This can happen in personal crisis, relationship crisis, burn out, financial crisis, and in the approach of dying. We sense that our defenses are being cracked from the outside. We think that something or someone is against us, and we have to fight for our very survival. Sometimes we win, often we don't. This is a rough time, and one that brings many people to therapy.

Warmth also comes when we are touched by love. Like Mojud from the Sufi story, we get a taste of love-presence. The shimmering green light of love does something to us. We feel seen, recognized. In this recognition we are miraculously transported from being a poor government employee into being a "man or woman of great prospects." We get turned on. The inner fire warms up and the outer ice starts melting. We feel new, wondrous possibilities, like colored lights appearing in the drab grey world of our control system.

We sense, even if vaguely, a good place inside our selves that is both new and very familiar. We realize that we have the opportunity to respond from this deeper place, that we can be more true than the created self. We are willing to let go of defenses, to meet our feelings, to move with the situation we are in. We open into the inner river and jump in.

Getting wet is not something we have to do; it is something that we want to do.

Even though we don't know what we are getting into, we jump in. We let our selves be washed, taken.

Love makes us crazy.

Therapy and Meditation: The Merging

Meditation builds Presence. Not that it creates something new or gives us another new skill to add to our old identities. What meditation does is slowly relax us back into contact with our authentic, original state of being. It releases us from who we try to be and brings us back into who we are.

When such Presence is the ground under therapy, then the quality of therapy changes dramatically. This is the gift of Zorba the Buddha: therapy from a base of meditation, therapy in service of meditation.

Without meditation and its field of Presence, all we really know about our self is based on identity. We feel like we are somebody who is defined by a past identity. We are a product of our past. When this notion holds our basic sense of self, then working on our self naturally means making this self more secure. We want a bigger, better self that won't be disturbed again the way we have been disturbed in the past. However, when we are touched by Presence—either our own or from someone else—another potential opens. We sense a deeper ground inside. We sense a potential of our self which is very different from the potential of the identity place. We feel a pull into this new potential. We want to get to know that inner self. We are attracted to look inside, to recognize more of our self than what the identities allow.

In the Friend approach Presence is the key to therapy that melts the rigidity, the ice of all the identities that we are caught in. This is the way into our inner world. He we return into the flow of our own subjectivity.

Friend's Way Therapy

The water element's challenge is let go. Surrender. To release out of our holding patterns, and to flow with life's experiences. We can't do that while clinging to our inner rocks, our old identities. We can only do it in response to trust, to allowing the flow of something bigger than us. This something bigger will take us. At first we don't know if this is a good thing or not. Maybe it will take us home, maybe it will take us to foreign lands…how can we know? Of course, later on we realize that the river is our friend, and that it will take us according to its wisdom. Even so, releasing out of the known rock identity and sliding into the flow of the river is always something of an adventure.

With the Friend's therapy techniques, this jump into the river doesn't have to be traumatic. Going inside doesn't have to be a fearful, life-threatening jump into the unknown. In fact, if we learn some basic techniques for being with our feelings, then we realize that we can actually float or even swim in our inner river. We quit resisting the pull of the water. We trust where it takes us. As we learn to be with our inner experience, as we learn how it opens and transforms, we find joy within our self.

When we have the skills to be in contact with our self, this self is not the barrier to spiritual growth. It is a system that has its architecture, its doors and passage ways. Actually it is a system of exquisite intelligence. When we learn to face the inner stress, confusion, emotion and such, then the inner doors are not so difficult to open. In fact, they seem to open all by themselves.

In The Friend's way, understanding grows. One of the fruits of this understanding is an appreciation that the River doesn't mind having its rocks. In fact, it is the play of water on the rocks that give each river its distinct character. Rivers wash rocks and rocks make music out of the water.

In the Friend's way, the play of rocks and river turns into a rhythm. That rhythm is holding, owning our present state, and releasing, letting go into the flow. We learn how to go into our experience and hold it. We accept and feel whatever emotional state is present. We offer it our body and our breath and our gentle attention. We learn its truth by allowing such a meeting, by actively participating in it without judgment. This inevitably leads into a relaxation. We aren't tensing against our selves; we are accepting and actively participating with these selves. In this relaxation, we can release our holding and ask, "If I let go here, what is true? Is this state I am in my full truth or is there something more true?" Here the meditative training takes over. While therapy gives us the skills to hold and explore our experience, meditation gives us the trust to release into a deeper level of truth. Meditators are familiar with the gaps between known experiences. They have experience in letting go of an old experience and waiting for a new one to form.

The techniques of holding and letting go play with each other in rhythms, like a river falling over its rocks.

We realize our inner dynamism. There is a flow of intelligence that takes us through our inner architecture. This inner flow is highly intelligent. It flows towards love as surely as the river heads to the ocean. We don't have to work to get inside, we simply let go and the inner river takes us there.

Example of Friend in Therapy
Here is a hypothetical example of how the Friend's way works.

Let's say that William comes for a session because of

relationship issues. He says that he and his partner are not connecting as deeply as they used to, and he misses it. He also says that when he is disturbed this way, he tries to meditate but ends up thinking a lot and only somewhat less disturbed than before he began to meditate.

When he is allowed to speak his mind freely, something starts relaxing already. When he begins to feel the Presence of the therapist, then his attention shifts from "her" as a problem to looking inside himself. As he does so, he realizes he doesn't like himself when he is angry, and that there is anger with his relationship. If he can feel the Presence field of the therapist here, then he doesn't get stuck in blaming himself for the anger. He doesn't find a locked door that says, "Bad Person Inside." He doesn't stand in judgment on himself. Instead, he can go into the anger place and explore it with an open mind. That may mean moving or verbalizing or making sounds that are true to the experience of the anger.

There are many different ways to explore the inner world, and usually one of them will appear—as if by magic—from his sincere determination. As he does, a lot of energy is released and a fresh sense of aliveness returns.

The aliveness itself starts to feel good. His body opens to it. It doesn't hold down the old feelings, it doesn't try to control and negate what is there. It "takes off its clothes and jumps in the river." When it does it finds more aliveness returning.

If the aliveness is allowed it turns into expression. The anger is a hardened form of something basic that wasn't able to communicate. In the aliveness, the hardness of the anger melts and the intention of the communication becomes clearer. The delicacy and vulnerability that were protected in the anger's hardness then reveal themselves. In the delicate, vulnerable part is an innocent, clear urge for communication and connection. This innocent urge for communication has been seriously wounded in early child years, so in later life it is guarded. In the aliveness of the moment and the Presence field of the therapist, the innocent communication is encouraged to return.

It does. William will likely fall into a deeper emotion. The anger had protected him, and is it releases, he discovers what is even more true. In this deeper emotion he usually falls into a much younger identity; he falls into a time of being small and helpless and vulnerable. If he is allowed to see this identity, then he realizes that he is carrying an old hurt from the past, and still projecting that the present situation will be a repeat of this old hurt.

If William is encouraged to simply stay present with himself here, he will come into a natural meditation. His inner river is flowing freely and true. In this natural meditation he will sense the goodness of himself. He will also be able to see where his problems came from. This seeing will be simple and clear and without judgment. Staying simple and open here, he will find that his natural intelligence switches on. The solutions to his problem will arise from within. These solutions will be offered out of his present intelligence, they will reflect the truth of his inner nature.

A deeper sense of rest and goodness are likely to arise. William can sit in his chair and experience a profound sense of goodness within himself and in his life as a whole. He realizes he is not afraid.

There is a strong trust quality. He may feel love. He may appreciate the humor of the situation. He is likely to feel grateful...even to his partner. He is grateful for releasing anger, for recovering the vulnerability that it was protecting. He is grateful to be at home in vulnerability.

He is surprised to find the way his deeper intelligence responds when he approaches it with vulnerability. He realizes he is learning to trust and like himself. He makes an inner promise to stay present with himself, to give himself the quality of attention that opens his inner world.

Zorba goes Zen
When Zorba's aliveness meets Zen awareness, a new world of possibilities unfolds.

Zorba is simplicity and aliveness. He is not about to be cowed by any "Seeker" who wants him/her to be still and well behaved. He won't be put in a box labeled "Ego" and then scrutinized with distant eyes. He doesn't want to walk around in a suit and tie like he is going to Sunday School every day.

Zorba demands attention. In fact, the Zorba part of us demands more than just attention. He demands Identification. Zorba shouts, "This is me! Like it or not, Here I am!" Zorba won't allow us to split away and deny him. He invites us into his passion, grabs our hand and takes us into a dance so total that we become one.

When Zorba is so insistent, Buddha has a choice: he can retreat into holding old precepts and morality about how to behave, or he can open to the situation and bless it with his awareness.

Usually Buddha is up to the challenge. He says, "You can feel whatever you want, you can be alive in any way that you like. Just be aware in it. Anything goes, as long as you are aware in it. Aware means watching, aware means asking, "Who am I" even as you dance, sing, cry, or laugh."

This combination brings pure gold to the inner world.

First, it supports us to be actively engaged in our feeling world. To not ignore what is going on under the surface, but to welcome it and see it as a deeper form of our intelligence which is trying to communicate.

We learn to be open to our feeling states, and to let the feelings touch us, to allow them to get under our skin and awaken us and provoke some kind of response.

Zorba is not afraid of feeling in this way. In fact, this kind of feeling is what he eats for breakfast. He loves it. What the Buddha brings to it is awareness. Awareness shows us a new way with feeling, that we have often been uncreative with our feelings. In awareness we discover how we have tried to manage our feelings, how we react to our feelings, how we have tried to control our selves. In other words, how blind we can be when we are fully aroused in feeling.

Zorba the Buddha is a way of keeping our light on inside even when we are submerged in sadness and raging in anger. It is a way of staying present within our feeling world, keeping a sense of awakeness and curiosity about what is going on even as we are consumed in it.

There is a constant curiosity: "Is this true? What is more true? What is even more real? What if I open my heart to being in this feeling, right now?"

When we dare to explore inside our feeling world, we recover the alive intelligence that is in our feeling world. This is very precise, dynamic intelligence which is passionately trying to find a new way in the present situation. It is the burst of love intelligence which comes from our heart.

Usually we don't have this experience with our feelings. Usually emotions take us into feeling separate, alone, misunderstood, clumsy, in rage, in fear of other such stuff. Not so nice places to be.

In therapy situations I see that feelings take us back into the felt sense of being younger. In that younger place, we don't feel empowered, in fact we feel helpless and that the feelings we are having are being provoked out of our helpless state. Obviously we don't like such a feeling of being in feelings. In the child times, we were controlled and judged for giving in to our feelings, and even in adult times, we regret it when we are provoked by feelings big or small.

We feel threatened by feelings and have to find some way to avoid being overwhelmed by them. We are wary of the feeling world and what it brings us, especially when it brings us out of the box of who we should be and puts us in the wilderness of who we really are.

It is so direct. So sharp. So naked.

As in the Mojud story, we "take off our clothes and jump in the River," not knowing if someone will save us or not.

The first learning that comes with feelings is that we don't have to contract with them, we don't have to freeze. No matter how strong the feeling is, we have options. We can explore what we feel. We can be curious about it: we can get to know it. We can allow its intrinsic movement to flow through our bodies.

It is said that when Buddha was nearing his enlightenment, all the forces of Mara, the king of Unconsciousness, attacked him. When Heaven's sexy girls came dancing and Mara's arrows of outrageous fortune were slung at him, he kept his awareness with his breath and touched the ground with his left hand. He said, "The earth is my witness."

In a similar way, we learn to stay with our breathing and feel our contact with our body and the ground around us even as we go into feeling. This keeps us here and now with it, and doesn't allow us to regress too far into the contracted ways of being in feeling that protected us as children. We stay here and now, breathing, in touch, and the earth quality of being here and now will protect our light of awareness even in the strongest challenges.

We recognize our self as having a feeling, not as being a small child overwhelmed by our feeling.

When we are settled in exploring feelings, we can go a step further into taking ownership of them. We can understand the feelings as our own. We don't fall into the trap of feeling helpless or blaming others for what we feel: "You made me angry. You made me afraid." We hold the anger and fears as our own creation, our own way of relating to the situation we are in.

As we said before, these ways of relating will be very primitive, clumsy, crude, and embarrassing at first. If we have the encouragement to not run from them, the basic intelligence of the feelings will emerge from the crude, clumsy wrapping they are in.

The quality of the feelings starts changing. Our feelings are no longer hard, fixed objects that stand between us and the outside world. They are not solid things that will last forever. They are intense, fluid energies that can flow in many directions. One direction is out towards others, another direction is in towards the deeper layer of our selves. In either case, allowing the feelings to flow brings the awareness that they will change. They are essential fluid energies. They will become more true, more real when allowed to change.

When we follow the inner flow, the feelings guide us into our resources; they bring us into the places inside our selves where there is the native intelligence and strength to handle whatever we are facing.

In this recognition, we can communicate creatively with the energy form of feelings. We can ask, "What is this feeling telling me?" "If I let go into it, how would I move? What would I say?"

We find that our feelings are intense attempts to communicate. Communicate something meaningful and precious to us. They have force and power because this preciousness is not being seen, not being allowed...like a river that is flowing in a tight place.

If a river is too controlled, it gets wild. If a river is dammed up, it will eventually break down the dam in a massive flood. If we control our feeling world too much, the inner river is turbulent or stagnant. We have no way of understanding what we are so wanting to communicate. Being aware in feeling means that we open into the feelings and allow them to widen out. As the feelings lose pressure, they reveal the preciousness of their desire to communicate. We can find the precision of our emotional intelligence when it is allowed to flow freely.

Practicing this way of being with our feelings, again and again, we find a fearless sense of intimacy growing within our self. We know that any place we start can lead us into deeper connection with our self, and in that deeper connection with our self, we find invaluable resources waiting for us there. We find the basic goodness of who we are. We find tremendous strength in this.

We also discover that our anger and fear and sadness can bring us into better contact with the world around us. Our feelings can make us more realistic, more in touch with other people. We can break through many of the conventions of how we are supposed to relate and discover the truth of our connections with other people. This is an enormously rewarding discovery as it dawns on us that we are able to discover a world of rich and intimate connections with other people by following the flow of our feeling world.

Further, in recognizing how difficult it is for us to be present with our own emotions, we have a good handle on what it is like for others. It is not easy for us; it is not easy for our friends and enemies either. We are all trying to communicate some very deep and important things but caught in very crude, unskillful forms of relating to our own feeling.

We don't know the depth and truth of what we feel until we make the journeys to go there...we are all caught in the same struggles with distrusting our feeling world and in these struggles, we are missing its essential intelligence.

And love.

In the Zorba the Buddha quality of being in feeling and remaining awake to it, we rescue our feeling world from the past tense and bring it into the present tense. We don't fall into the trap of sensing our feeling as replays of past childhood wounds, we find the ground to stand in our feeling and see how it is clearing the way for very skilful communication and connection in the present moment. We feel empowered by our feeling, even if the beginning of this empowerment is a sense of fear or sadness or some other scruffy looking starting place. We know that whatever we start with is fine. It simply means our river is now flowing.

And, once our River is flowing, it will move in the direction of love.

The River

A river enjoys the play of its water over its rocks. Even so, as the river flows further downstream, it joins other rivers. It becomes wider. Slower. The older rivers lose their rocks. They find their grace. They find a depth that they can rest into. They are less identity bound to the place where they have come from. They are more like the ocean where they are heading.

These same things happen inside us as we be-friend our water. The turbulence of our feeling world settles. We find the grace of our natural movement. In that grace is trust and depth and a deep certainty of our returning home.

Fire

Once there was a fresh spring high in the mountains. Its waters were pure, clean, and good.

As they ran downhill, these waters became a brook, which joined with other brooks until there was a stream. Several streams made a river, and the river was proud in its journey out of the mountains down towards the sea.

When the river came out of the mountains it entered into a plain. In the flatlands the flow slowed down, and the river widened. The water lost its crystal clear quality and became colored with the mud of the earth.

Eventually the river entered a place of great sand dunes and stopped altogether.

For the first time it felt hesitant. It didn't know what to do. If it went forward, it would simply be absorbed into the sandy wastes. If it stayed still, it would become increasingly stagnant. And, of course, there was no way back. The river couldn't believe that it had come so far to be simply a dull, muddy pool trapped in the sands. It couldn't believe that its guidance had betrayed it so badly. The river fell into deep confusion and helplessness. It did not know where it could go. There was nothing it could do, no way out.

The longer it stood, the more stagnant it became. It felt deep grief in seeing its once pristine waters turning into a dull swamp.

Days and months passed by with no change. The once flowing river fell further into deep despair.

It tried to pray, but there was no answer. It became angry and cursed, but again there was no response. It felt pity for itself, but the stagnation just settled in even more deeply. The situation felt utterly hopeless. The river lost heart.

At this bleak point came a gift from the beyond. The Sufis say that the whisper came from the sands themselves. The river wasn't quite sure. However it did hear a whisper.

Listening a little more intently, the river heard the message: "If you let yourself dissolve in the sun, the winds will pick you up and carry you over the sands, and drop you in the sea."

The stream turned river was quite confused. Everything had been so clear and so easy on its journey down the mountains. Now it was stagnant and muddy and had no hope of reaching the ocean except by following the whisper of its enemy, the sands: to dissolve and the winds will carry you. The river was proud of itself. At least it had been proud of itself.

Dissolve all of that? Give it up? All it had ever known was to run free and let gravity guide it. It had never dreamed that it could go up as well as down. How could it trust that it would be changed back to water again? How would it know that the winds would carry it to the ocean?

The river gathered heart and offered itself to the sun. It let the sun's fire turn it to vapor, and the vapor climbed into the clouds in the sky.

The winds carried the clouds far over the sands to the distant ocean. There, it is said, the clouds dumped tears of joy into the sea.[8]

Fire Eyes

In the Sufi Story "The Tale of the Sands," another element arises to continue the journey of the water. This is Fire. Water brings us into flowing and trusting. Fire takes us into transformation.

When we release out of the water world we come into fire. Here we are confronted with seeing more clearly into others and our self.

This is not always an easy place to be. In the water world, we have the luxury of creating emotional reactions as ways of processing difficulties. In the fire world we don't have this luxury. We see directly. We see the attitudes and identities behind our feelings. We see the thoughts and attitudes which give rise to the feelings we have.

We see many things which have been hidden away. Most of these were hidden away for good reason. They are not very logical or pretty or nice or looking good. When we come into some of the old, musty rooms of our inner architecture, and we put on the light, the first things we are likely to see are cobwebs and cockroaches. Maybe we even see a rat or two scurrying around.

When we drop into fire, the world is not so cozy as the water has been. There is intensity and aloneness and the jagged edges of a reality that we simply have to see for what it is. As fire brings us to transformation, the old, familiar self is challenged in even deeper ways that through water.

Our vehicle for journeying here is Seeing. If the seeing is good and true, then we are guided into clarity. In that clarity, many of our old assumptions about who we are and what our life is about will be re-examined.

Amsterdam Fire

Around four in the afternoon the street lights switch on for the Amsterdam winter darkness. Traffic starts piling up and a sleeting rain drizzles down more often than not. For those who might look outside for joy and comfort, the early night doesn't offer much.

It was another one of those days where November dulls down into the dreary sameness that will carry on until March. I was in the meditation room and unwinding from the day's work.

I was touched again. Being with others brings vulnerability, and in that vulnerability I knew that something of my own was knocking on my door this evening. After a full day's work, I felt tired and lazy. The instinct was to curl up on the floor and nap. However, I knew that this would only awaken me to a colder and darker world later.

Whatever it was that wanted to come through, I wanted to face it this time. I stood up and asked for the feeling to come. My body responded with little swaying movements and a tremor in the left leg. I coaxed this movement with a gentle breathing out and gave permission for my body to flow as it wanted to.

Soon my whole body was shaking and through that shaking grief broke through. The grief opened a long, dark corridor of empty, lonely feeling. It felt like there must be twenty little jail cells off of this corridor, each of them holding a sad, lonely, guy from many different times.

I thought the grief and darkness might overwhelm me.

Instead, the shaking became stronger. As the body was allowed to move, I became even more in the present tense. I realized was no longer overwhelmed with grief.

I was now something Fierce. This night it was different. I simply wasn't afraid anymore. I didn't have to escape or blame or fear or deny… I was something more true than all of that. I was just a pure fire of intensity, something like a Polar Bear, 500 kilograms of raging intensity.

The ice was my home, the water my hunting place. I could eat sadness and fear and loneliness for breakfast.

A few moments later, instead of a bear's roar, I heard a voice. My own voice.

"I am here now."

I heard it, felt it, realized…I am here now. Angry, red…and here.

I became very alert. This "I" was both very new and also very old and familiar. It had a sense of peace in it, a quality of integrity. It wasn't a feeling. It was more certain, more true than feeling. It was like a kind of Presence that is wider and deeper than feeling.

The fierceness remained, but it didn't have a fight attached to it. There was just a fire that was burning without reason for it to burn. It was simply a burning of itself. The intensity was of something awakening, like a bear coming out of hibernation.

I took my heavy winter coat and headed out into the night. I promised to let this polar bear walk until it settles inside me. I wanted to walk it, feel it, look with its eyes, hear its voices…I promised not going to dress it up or subdue it in any way. I was glad for the dark, cold, rainy night. It was a perfect hunting ground for a polar bear on fire.

Fifteen minutes down the street, I felt the fire extending in front of my body like a red orange aura. I was invincible. Then I heard a voice say, "Nishant, you have this red field all around you…but look inside that field. What is different about you just because you have your red fur on?"

I was surprised. I realized I had been looking out with all my intensity and had neglected to be also looking in.

I looked inside. The intensity of the looking took me straight to the core. Nothing was different. I was the same guy I had been all day. The anger was a set of clothes I had on. To all appearances I looked different in it, but in the fire of the night I saw that I am the same guy inside no matter what I feel, no matter how I look.

"Nothing is different now," I replied. "Just me."

Another twenty minutes of walking the voice came back again.

"See the red orange field around you. That is your anger."

"Got it," I said.

"What is inside that right now?" the voice asked.

I looked again.

"I am pretty calm right now, cool even. I feel peaceful and there is a dark quiet."

"OK," said the voice. "Which is more real?"

Again I was surprised. I looked out to the fire around me and felt fierce. I looked into the core of me and felt cool, relaxed, even a little playful by now. I had never seen so clearly.

"It all depends on where I look," I said. "If I look out, that makes the anger real. If I look in, the coolness is more real. Whatever I feed with my attention is what grows."

Later that night I am peaceful and in front of a fireplace. The intensity has transformed into a warm glow, like a fire that is not hungry right now. It is peaceful. There is no aggression left in it.

"I am here now" returns. I am here now. I feel the red, the pain, and the orange linked into a rainbow of experience. Being in one of them doesn't make the other less real. They are all connected, all part of a bigger something that turns on and off with my attention.

"I am here now."

Fully here. So this is what it is like. Alone but not separate.

I look around the apartment. There is a simple, quiet beauty here tonight.

I become curious. What is it to look inside with these same eyes?

I relax my eyes and come back to sensing the breath in my belly. It has a slow, steady rhythm tonight. Different visions form in front of my eyes. I see images from my past slowly taking shape in front of me. Some of them are nice and good, and many of them are not. Each time I react either for or against one of these images, I hear a voice saying, "Just see it... Remember, don't react, just see it."

As this process continues for some time, I also know that I am looking at these things, that there is an observer who is more real than the images that he sees. I sense into this observer. The intensity is around him, but he himself is not intense. He is hugely spacious and in that spaciousness he is capable of absorbing anything without the contracting to it.

A tear forms in my eye. It rests there for a short while, and then slides down my cheek. There is something so precious in this observer inside; I feel this moment like a reunion with a dear friend. The seeker, searcher self is quiet now. There is a quality of seeing in its place. That seeing is without hunger or passion or judgment. My eyes are full of gratefulness and that gratefulness is what is looking out through them.

I realize that over the day's journey I have passed through a transition. My journey started in intense feeling and was then guided into journeying by seeing. I was being taken from Water into Fire, and in that Fire I was being taught to see.

And to Be.

Seeing

Seeing seems natural, simple, and easy. After all, we are doing it all the time. We think we see fine, even if that means putting on our lenses to read a book. Still, for seeing things of the inner world, for seeing into the nature of who we are, we are almost blind.

Why does it take a meditator years and years and years of sitting in front of a blank wall in order to develop clear seeing? Why is it so difficult for ordinary people to see something as basic as the goodness inside our self?

Why is it that we have very little perception of who we are? Our unique individuality?

When we are with friends and lovers, how much of them do

we see?

Clear seeing challenges something basic to the way we live.

With a little attention to it, we realize that our seeing is hardly the relaxed, open process that we think it is. Our seeing is clouded with memory, selective attention, focus distortions, and reactivity.

Our seeing isn't a passive reflection of the world around us. It is more a highly activated filtering system. Of course, not only is this happening with the world around us, it carries over into the world inside us as well. We don't mirror our self; we react and filter our vision of our self.

In the therapy world we work through many wounded aspects of the self. One of the deepest of these is the feeling of not being seen. We didn't feel seen when we were children, and to a large degree, we don't feel seen even to the present time.

As children, we didn't feel seen because our parents were busy making us into the person they thought we should be, and often that was more important than supporting us to be the person that we truly are. As adults, we continue this process, only it is not the parents who are making us who they think we should be, it is us who is doing this to our selves. We are so busy with managing our self to be the person we think we should be that we don't see who it is that we really are.

Even our own eyes turn heavy, knowledgeable, and judgmental when they look inside. These eyes are reacting against so many things which don't fit the image that they wants us to fit.

The inner being is a very persistent fellow, and it keeps trying to emerge our whole lives long. But it cannot emerge very fully to eyes that are not ready to see and accept it. As long as we are resisting what is inside us, then the truth of that resisted element will not be seen. The fire door opens when we are willing to sacrifice what we would prefer to see, and be willing to see what is really true.

The inner world withers from mental or emotional aggression. If we have passed through water, then we have the kindness that develops through intimacy. The lessons of the water bring safety to the unfolding of the fire. The water tempers judgment, especially the kind we learned to control our selves.

Looking and Looking Inside

How do we look at our selves? What quality of attention do we bring inside?

Before we answer those questions directly, let's look at looking. How do we do it?

We learn our seeing skills when we are young, and unless there is very compelling reason to do so, we don't change the way we see very much as we go through our lives. As children, we are dependent on the world around us. If we see something good, then we relax and feel good. If we see something bad or disturbing, then we are disturbed. What we see has the power to make us feel good or feel bad. We are intimately linked to what we see. We don't question the nature of our I-Thou relating with the world: the Thou has the power to make our I react.

We experience our seeing as a passive thing. We simply react to what we see.

As we grow older, we continue to put attention on the objects we see with the assumption that these objects have the power to make us happy or sad. In the I-Thou world, Thou still has the power. We relate as victims to what we see: "You made me happy," or "The team made me angry."

This kind of seeing carries over to our internal vision as well. We look inside ourself in the same way. When we see something likeable in our self, we think it makes us good. Conversely, when we see something we don't like, then we think we are bad.

Because what we see inside tells us who we are, we naturally react to these things. We fight against bad news and we welcome good news. Good news takes us up and bad news rolls us down again. This roller coaster accelerates when we are reactive to it—when we want to be up and good and when we resist being down and "bad."

In that constant stream of reactions we spend a lot of energy trying to manage what we see so that it will give us the news that we want. We create magical mind mirrors and say, "Mirror mirror on the wall, tell me I am the fairest of them all."

Our seeing ability learns to defend our security by selectively allowing some things in and keeping others out. We learn to not see. We learn to shut down our visual field or go out of focus when things are too much. We see what we want to see, and we don't see what would disturb us.

This defense system works its wonders, but, like all the other defense systems, creates another set of problems later in life.

The self reveals itself in many ways. Some of these ways will be labeled "good," and many of them won't. Some days we are bright and shiny, but just as surely there are other days when we are sad, or lonely, or angry or lost. In the Sufi world, God is known to have 100 names. Some of these are most wondrous and praiseworthy, and many of them speak of things like loneliness and desolation. In our inner world, we also have at least 100 names. But to the child's eyes, only three or four are likely to be "good."

When we follow this pattern with our self, then we invariably end up in reaction with what is being revealed. We see the angry one as a bad, or we see the sad one as a threat, or we hide the hurt one.

In such an atmosphere, the self doesn't unfold very much. When we only see what we want to see about our self, the fullness of who we are is not welcomed. We stay on the surface of our personality and don't penetrate very deeply into the truth of who we are. The True Nature of our sadness doesn't open into judgment and rejection. The deep roots of our self lie undiscovered by eyes that are afraid of the dark.

Seeing Skills

As we understand that the **way** we see determines **what** we see, we realize the way we look inside determines who we will find there. Some eyes will take us in while other eyes will keep us out.

If we are to know more clearly who we are, then we need a new way of looking at our self. A new set of skills is required for the precision and understanding that fire opens.

Following are three of the more useful skills for seeing: "Warm Eyes," "Wide Eyes," and "The Open Flash of Seeing." Each of these skills offers a way for normal seeing to turn into genuine in-sight.

Warm Eyes

Warm eyes are connected to a warm heart. In the warm eyes skill, we understand that the way we see affects what we see.

We realize that the child's version of seeing has kept us dependant on what we see as if the power is external. In the warm eyes skill, we awaken to the power of warmth that comes from our vision; that our eyes can transmit warmth when they see. When we transmit warmth from our eyes to people, plants, animals, objects, internal objects, our selves...then that warmth affects what is seen.

With warm eyes, the quality of seeing touches others palpably. When we are seen by warm, accepting eyes, we feel it. We respond to being "well seen" in the same way that we respond to being "heard" by someone who really listens to us. While fearful judging eyes bring forth a limited response from us, warm eyes invite us to be who we are.

Warm eyes are not blind. Such eyes can see our deficiencies. Even so, the way they see these deficiencies actually transforms them. There is no need fight or denial. There is simply acknowledgment. If we can join in the simple acknowledgement, then the struggle against our selves relaxes. We find that we can look at our self with warmth even when that particular self isn't one of our favorites.

In my therapy practice, one of the magic questions is "What happens if you open your heart to yourself here? What happens if you open your heart to being afraid, or lost, or sad, or stressed out?"

In these questions is the invitation to look at the self and its experiences with warm eyes. It works wonders. Whatever had seemed to be the source of the complaint, when looked at with warm eyes, isn't such a monster. The fear or sadness or stresses are not the problem they had appeared to be. A new seeing happens, and in that new seeing comes a new understanding of our self. In the warmth of this new understanding is also a new sense of appreciation for who we are.

Feelings and Facts

As we practice with warm eyes, we start to distinguish between feelings and facts. In the kindness of warm eyes, the perception of feelings and facts clarifies, something like cream coming off of milk. We can see clearly which are which. Facts are like mountains. They just are the way they are. Feelings are our attitudes about these facts. A fact is something like "I am sick." A feeling is "I'm miserable when I'm sick." In this example sickness is a fact and the misery and miserable sense of self is feeling. In our confusion, we are likely to see these two things as one thing, and say something like "Being sick makes me miserable."

Until we start to see more clearly, we unconsciously link feelings with facts, as though these facts determine our feeling. We think changing the facts will make us happier. When we can see more clearly, we realize that happiness is not a product of the facts, it is a result of the way we deal with these facts. We understand that the better use of time and attention is to work with the feelings.

With warm eyes, we can observe, "What is true about what I am feeling?" In that observing quality we can see that most feelings carry the imprint of past experience. Often deep feeling brings us back to the deep feelings we had as a child. With warm observation we can ask, "Is this true that I am so young? Are these feelings accurate to the situation I am in?"

This way of seeing is hot. It brings us out of very protected habits of emotional behavior. This is a challenging step already. However, in the light of the seeing, we are able to discover our present tense self, to see who is often hidden behind the emotional patterns we are in.

In the present tense self we have a fresh, warm intelligence to deal with the facts in our lives. We have creativity and love and patience and the so many more things that come as we take responsibility to be here as adults.

When we are ready to open our eyes and see.

Wide Eyes

The second seeing skill is called Wide Eyes.

In the Tibetan meditation tradition, yogis who practiced meditation for years and years sooner or later develop "The View." The View is a wide, expansive way of looking that has the ability to stay centered even while seeing all the details. The View carries a sense of expansiveness with it; we can see hundreds of mountains at the same time as we can see one.

Wide eyes is a vision skill that is a modern adaptation of this tradition.

With wide eyes, we learn to look without holding on to a focus point. We stay loose and relaxed. We don't go looking for any special details. We allow whatever wants to come into our field of attention to walk in and be welcome. We are receptive and patient. When one item shows itself in our field of attention, we acknowledge it, and observe it, and relax into a wider field again and see if there is anything else that also wants to come in. Our attention stays open for whatever wants to present itself.

This is a different kind of looking than how we are trained. In school and professional training, we are taught to focus our attention in order be more effective. We gain power over information by dividing it into small bits and then focusing on the small bits that we want handle. This attitude becomes such a habit that we tend to repeat the act of focusing whenever we meet challenges, either inside our selves or with others. Through the emphasis on focusing, we learn to see the leaves on a tree and can lose track of the forest around it.

This style of looking is wonderful for solving scientific problems, but it isn't so effective for matters of the heart. The heart doesn't work through divide and conquer mentality; the heart works by embracing and unifying. Excessively focused vision is not natural to the way our heart sees. We lose the warm heart that supports the warm eyes that can reveal what is truly important. If we look hard, we will never see the whole person. We will get some details of this and that, but we can't get the living wholeness of a person by studying them. However, when we relax and ground our looking in our own presence, then we can be taken into a place where wholeness reveals itself.

Looking from a place of relaxed presence, we don't see a collection of details that compete with each other for importance. Instead we see something more fundamental. We have a view that can embrace the living wholeness of a person.

As we become accustomed to wide eyes, we also begin to see the context of things more clearly. We can see more clearly the way of appropriate action.

For example, a client may say, "I have fear."

If we can receive this with wide eyes, then we can also see if this fear stands alone, or if it is part of a bigger network of things. In that network we can see if the fear is connected to anger or if it is connected to family conditioning or if it has a psychological, physical, or spiritual root to it...many details will come to fill in around this fear if we are able to be receptive and wide enough to allow them in.

As details reveal themselves to this kind of attention, we don't make a big deal out of picking and choosing which is most valuable. We simply stay relaxed and the right ones will announce themselves.

Within our selves it is the same. When we recognize our own fear, we don't harden into a strong focus on it. We don't bring an aggressive way of looking to it. We stay wide with our vision. We are available to see what is under the fear, what is behind the fear, where the fear comes from, what it is trying to turn into, how this fear is carrying remnants from the past but actually is a spark of intelligence trying to communicate something in this present moment. We allow these details to announce themselves to us when and how they will. We don't run them through a set program or put them in order. We deeply trust that the intelligence of the fear will reveal to us exactly what it is seeking and when that is acknowledged it will guide us into what—if anything—is next.

Some people get in trouble with wide eyes because wide eyes remind them of trauma situations. In active trauma there is an exaggerated wide field of vision. If the trauma doesn't clear from our body, then there is a tendency to carry this exaggerated wide field of vision for extended periods of time before it collapses into a very contracted field of vision.

Even for normally traumatized people, it can be scary to look without subjecting the object of our attention to a strong field of focus.

A key to support wide eyes is conscious breathing. By breathing through our nose into the center of our lower belly or the center of our heart, then we can actually feed the fire quality inside us with our own breath.

As we stay in touch with the fire, then the fear is a secondary phenomenon that doesn't dominate our situation, but rather adds elements of sensitivity and compassion to it. When the breath is fine tuned, then there is also a warm sense of humor, a feeling of an inner smile that greets whatever we see.

This kind of breathing will be comforting and centering. It will give the support we sometimes need to look in a way that doesn't impose our sense of order on the person (or self) that we are seeing, but rather holds a wide field of vision for the other's intelligence to reveal itself.

In wide eyes, the self isn't the person that we had tried so hard to be. It isn't the one that we had expected. There is more to all of us than we had known. In the View, there is no opinion about any of the self that unfolds to our wide vision. Seen with the eyes of love, the self goes beyond the world of judgment. It returns into the open field of nature, where, like each animal that walks free and wild, the self has its own intrinsic grace and beauty.

Open Flash of Seeing

The open flash of seeing is an adaptation of the Zen tradition.

In Zen meditation, meditators sit facing a wall. Nothing happens except the play of our own minds. As we fall into this situation, we find a very busy mind taking over. There is the mind stuff of memory, feeling, expectation, hoping, fearing and clinging and more. It takes quite some time, but sooner or later just as the mind rises up it also settles down. As the mind games settle down, there is simply being at home with progressively clear seeing. A big feature of this clear seeing is the ability to see things fresh, as if we are continually discovering things for the first time.

In the open flash of seeing our eyes enjoy discovering. We see each thing as if we are seeing it for the first time. We constantly discover the world around us. Every time we look, we see something new, something different from what we had just seen before. This is the kind of seeing that the Zen master Suzuki Roshi referred to as "Beginner's Mind."[9]

In the open flash of intelligence, we are happy to return to being beginners, to discovering what is revealing itself to us in the present moment. We enjoy the play of not-knowing what we are going to find.

In my therapy practice this kind of seeing works wonders. It allows me to meet my client in a moment where the past and the future are secondary—I can see the person who is here with me right now. This person who is here right now holds the key to whatever needs to happen. Relating directly with him or her begins an almost magical process of recognizing and being with a person in the act of unfolding.

In a single hour's session I meet at least five different aspects of a client as they appear and talk to me. The one who walks in the door is not the one who is sitting in the chair ten minutes later. The person who brings fear often turns into a person who is hiding their anger. A person who presents with anger often opens up as a person who is protecting their hurt. As one part shows up and is welcomed, then another and another also come to join in. This leads to increasing levels of intimacy and truth as the self trusts to keep revealing more. I love this aspect of therapy. Each moment offers the possibility for a new discovery.

The open flash of seeing not only reveals new things; it takes us into a different dimension of time. We enter into the present tense so fully that it feels as though all time stops. We come into a state where the present moment is just it. This "it" has the potential of a past and the potential of a future, but in the reality of "it," there is also no sense of either past or future. Things are just what they are. They are not necessarily caused by anything in the past nor framed by some future destination. They just are here. We find this quality of being in the here and now enormously refreshing. We can slide out of our personal history and find a beingness that is independent of any history. In the Zen tradition, this is known as *returning to the source.*

Visual Koan

In Kyoto, Japan, there is a Zen temple with a famous rock garden. The temple is called Ryoanji. The whole temple is a statement of Zen beauty, but the garden is very special. This garden is a masterpiece with a secret. The garden is constructed as a visual koan, a visual puzzle to test your meditation. In this visual puzzle, there are 15 rocks set in a small graveled yard. No matter where you sit or stand, you can't see all of the rocks at the same time. You want to see them all and you can't. Try as you like, the stones are so precisely placed that no place will allow you to see the whole picture.

This visual Koan is something that you can't solve with your ordinary mind. Of course I tried every position and hoped that as a six foot westerner I could stand on my tip toes and see what the shorter Japanese Zen students would have missed. Unfortunately, it was simply too well made. I couldn't get it. Then, one day, I went there and instead of trying to see the whole garden, I gave up trying. I sat down, crossed my legs and looked softly at the space just in front of my eyes. I just relaxed into being in the presence of this garden and trusted that it would offer me what I was ready to receive.

This went on for more than a few changes of bus tours. Suddenly I was aware that my consciousness was floating high above my body, in fact it was hovering over the garden. I looked down, and from there I could see the whole garden. At last the garden had shown me how to see its secret. I had to laugh as the garden shared its beauty with me.

Years later, I realized that it is the same thing with people.

Seeing People

With the skills of Warm Eyes, Wide Eyes, and Open Flash of Seeing, we have a new way of seeing people.

We see the wholeness that is already here. We can appreciate the beauty and goodness of the person we are with. We feel the freshness of a beauty that has just this moment been displayed and discovered. We can see the dignity of the soul that sits inside the person who sits inside the body who sits inside this moment. We see the basic nature of a person. We appreciate it and love it and relate to it.

Of course that does not mean that we don't see the problems that the other person is bringing us. Or that we don't feel helplessness or fear or sadness as they journey into such places in our presence. But it does mean that we have known something more fundamental about the other person than the problems that they bring us. We have seen the basic ground of them, and can relate to the natural beauty of that person even as that natural beauty has been covered with distortions of all kinds.

My meditation teacher Osho once said that a good therapist is like a good potter. A potter makes clay pots by putting clay on a wheel and spinning the wheel. As the wheel spins, the potter has one hand inside to support the pot rising into the desired shape. The other hand is on the outside to trim away the rough edges. So it is that a good therapist has one hand supporting the inner growth of a person while the other hand is trimming away some of the rough edges.

With the seeing skills of Fire eyes, we see the inside of a person. We see how we can support that inside to rise up and be here. We see the core strengths of a person and the core goodness that is trying to find its way into living. Just simply seeing these things we can acknowledge them and offer them the kind of support that is very very rare in this life. We can genuinely support a person to be who they are and not push them into being who we think they should be.

Of course, this kind of relating is a hot place to be. In order to meet others in these fresh and open places, we have to drop into those same fresh and open places in our selves. We can't keep on the overcoat of our ego shell as we encourage someone else to drop theirs. We need to drop into the same openness that we are encouraging others to drop into. Here is also the key to getting to know our selves.

In such a way of being with others, we are brought into discovering our self as well. We become new to our self, and we find surprise and delight in what that self has to offer to the present situation. We don't know exactly what this self is going to say or how it is going to touch. In not knowing the other, we are open to our own creativity to unfold…to see who we are in this moment.

These kind of experiences can make even an Amsterdam November day something that is warm and exciting and full of mystery and promise.

Quality Attention

As we learn the art of bringing high quality of attention back towards others and our self, the self opens to that attention the way a flower opens to the sun. The self responds in kind to the way we touch it with our attention. It opens to us, just the same way that it opens to anyone who also offers us such attention.

With enough practice we learn to see light and goodness co-existing with fear and sadness. With warm and wide eyes, negative things and positive things are all part of the same continuum. No matter how difficult the journey we have been on—and believe me these journeys can be quite a nightmare—the basic quality of love goodness is still present within us.

True Nature

The gift of fire's vision is discovering the essential self—True Nature. The seeing skills of warm eyes, wide eyes, and open flash of vision bring a radically different perception of self. Together, they take us through the psychological frame that we have lived in, and introduce us to something even more funda-mental, the qualities of our Being.

In the fire's seeing we simply see what is here and now. We

drop through the apparent density of the remembered self and its psychological world. We see without old filters. It is not that we don't see the past, just that the past is less true than the present. In the fire of open seeing, the past doesn't have the same quality of reality as the Present.

This is like going from conventional Newtonian physics into the quantum state. When we drop through the psychological filters around our seeing, we discover a deeper Essential world. The field of Essence Being is a vast, unlimited, universal field. It is as empty as the Buddhists describe, and as lively as the dancing world of quarks, electrons, and photons that physicists find in open space.

Nothing is fixed there. Never was. Never will be. In other words, nothing has ever gone wrong, no scar has ever left a mark. No attempt at progress is needed to make this, or any, moment any better. In this world, there is no basis for fear, or guilt, or limitation, or suffering. Pain and pleasure will have their moments, but there are no traces left behind of either.

The essence world links us to a timeless state of Being. In the experience of this essence state, we sense Essence as more true than psychology.

Our present tense Being is more real than our psychological story. The essence world has a depth of beingness in it that we recognize as Reality. Tasting this reality is both wonderful and disturbing. The world we meet is a different world, and the being we are is a different being than what we have known for most of our lives. This newness takes some time integrating.

Summary: The Doors of Inner Seeing

In Fire we burn through the familiar sense of self. We see more clearly into what is inside us, and into the reality of our consciousness. If we can warmly see and allow our eyes to widen as we see, then we see more of the whole. We discover the context where things make sense. If we allow open flash seeing, then we discover the fresh truth of that lives in the musty old rooms of our psyche.

Ultimately this kind of seeing reveals True Nature. We discover an inner fire where the truth of "I am what I am" is also our personal reality. In that foundation, we can stay warmly present with our selves, even as some of the nasty things show up. The steady warmth of our eyes begins transforming even the oldest, darkest things inside us. This steady warmth melts the ice and allows the cobwebs and cockroaches and rats to revert back into their original true nature. What looks bad doesn't look bad after a while. Even the bad things have a context, a place where they make sense to a tender heart.

This kind of seeing brings understanding to whatever it sees. In the very quality of seeing so warmly, a process of redemption unfolds.

Space

In Water, the melting and flowing quality take us out of isolation. We learn the way to release held emotion and discover an inner flow of consciousness, a river which leads to the ocean of love.

With Fire comes intensity, clarity, and truth of Being: transformation of our basic sense of self. We burn off many images of who we are. The reality of our True Nature is more apparent.

From these two elements opens a third: Space.

A young Sufi student went to see the Master teacher in the Mosque. The young man asked, "Can you teach me about Freedom?"

The older man looked at him for a moment without saying anything. Then he walked to his study and came back with two birds in a golden cage.

He asked the student, "What do you see here?"

The student said, "I see two birds in a golden cage."

The teacher asked, "What would make these birds want to leave this cage? See, the cage is golden and they are honored in it. They are fed every day and given water and all the things that they could want."

The student replied, "Yes, it is so. But the cage is still a cage, even though it is golden. I don't think it makes that much difference to them how well decorated their cage is. A bird wants to fly and no golden cage is a good substitute. And as for the food, it is true that their body is cared for, but what about their soul? What about the part of them that knows the sky as their home? What about the trust that birds have that there will always be food when they are allowed to fly free?"

The teaching master said, "Tell me about this soul that even birds have."

The young student said, "I have come to you to learn about my soul, but even I can see that the soul of the bird is in the sky and not in a cage."

The teacher said, "Let's see." He opened the door to the cage and clapped his hands loudly. The startled birds flew out and began circling in the dome of the mosque as they looked for their way into open sky.

The Master asked the student, "Now, how do you get these birds out of the building?"

The student said, "Perhaps if we open a window and clap again, they will fly towards the light."

"Perhaps it is so," said the Master. "Try it."

The student climbed up to the first balcony, and opened two of the shuttered windows there. A broad beam of sunlight came down into the mosque. The student then went to the other side of the mosque, and shouted "Huk!" as he clapped his hands loudly. The birds saw their opportunity and swooped out.

The student watched them go and followed them into the blue sky.

He then turned towards the Master, but the Master wasn't there. Instead there was just an open door leading out to the street. The Master had already walked out, and all that was left behind was another ray of light streaming into the Mosque.

The Space Element

In the Zen tradition there is a saying, "In the beginning, rivers were rivers and mountains were mountains. Then, as the practice deepened, rivers weren't rivers and mountains weren't mountains any more. Finally, in the end, rivers are rivers again and mountains are mountains."

For someone who is journeying through Fire and Water, it is the same. As we come to know our selves better, life is not what we thought it was, and neither are we. Rivers are not rivers, and mountains are not mountains. Even more important, we are not who we thought we were.

The self we thought we were felt real, hard, fixed, both known and knowable. It carried a name and a history and lots of supporting evidence to tell us who we are. Our self has some good parts and some bad parts and we did our best with the good and we also did what we could to control the bad.

With the Friend's heartful awareness, we realize that the self feels hard and real because we are hard with it. Our critical attitude towards the self, our way of saying "good" and "bad" to the self creates the illusion that the self is a fixed thing. The way we stand outside the self creates the illusion that we are the director of a self. We labor under the illusion that two real, separate things exist. I and Thou has an inner projection as Me and Self. The antagonism between the subject and object continues.

As we learn the Friend quality, this same self returns the favor. It starts to open to us. The Zen bull that we have been chasing quits running away, and actually comes in our direction. We become aware of the aggression we have had towards our inner self, our bull. We have thought we were the good guy, the seeker self, looking to control the bad guy, the instinctual self. As we go further inside, we are not so sure anymore who is the good guy and who is the bad one. We really begin to wonder what is going on.

As we connect with our self even deeper, we realize that inside us are many identities, many different images of self. We are not just one or two. There are a multitude. We are a fighter, a lover, a seeker, a rebel, a good worker, a lazy bum, a good friend, someone who hates, someone who fears, someone who loves...Each time we take on an identity, we think, "This is me." "This is the real thing." And, each time we take on such an identity, the current identity feels empowered to suppress all the other identities. It is king for a day (or hour, or moment). We are continually in a parade of new kings for the day. Ultimately this is both confusing and hugely upsetting.

The good guys and the bad guys change on a daily basis. Each new self feels real, but in the light of patient awareness, each new self dissolves, just like some mirage in the desert. Each time an identity forms, we feel safe and secure in knowing what is going on. When they dissolve, when we are in-between identities, we are full of amorphous feeling and again, facing a desert without the mirage to guide us.

We see that our Seeker has always thought he was the good guy in search of the miscreant Zen bull. But in the wilderness that opens up, he sees that he is full of aggression and judgment and reaction against his Bull. He thinks he knows better than the Bull, but actually this is more bluff than reality. He thought his seeking was the way towards Truth, but actually, in the wilderness of the search, he realizes that this is not so. The seeker is as much a part of the problem as the solution.

It gets very shaky here. Mountains are not mountains and rivers are not rivers.

Who are we? Are we real? What is our Truth? If I am not

"Me," then who am I?

A very big, dark space begins to open up. This space is too big for any our identities to fill. At first it feels terrifying, way too big for our personality systems to handle.

First Encounters with Space

Here is a story of one of my first encounters with that big space.

Still awake, I'm looking at the sky at three in the morning on a humid August night in the southern USA. Tonight is the second night since my accident. The ground is hard under my sleeping bag. A few droning mosquitoes patrol the forest around me, and the night seems endlessly long. I look out into the dark night and its stars and it seems endless and cold. I don't know how to handle something so big and empty.

All I can do is wonder, "What happens to us when we die?" The question sends me looking out into the sky again. All that I find there is a big, cold, empty place that seemingly holds no inclination to comfort me or answer my question. I feel scared and drained. I wonder, "Does all of our heat and life activity just disappear out into that empty cold place?"

Two days ago I saved one of my Outward Bound students from going over a waterfall on the Chattooga River. The rescue went fine for her, but I was caught and taken over the falls.

In the whirlpool at the base of the falls I tumbled with no idea of how to escape. Eventually I passed out. The next thing I remembered was floating in a quiet pool somewhere further downstream. My body was limp as it hung over the life jacket. With a couple of feeble kicks, I propelled my way to the shore. I heard the buzzing of the flies and saw a few blades of grass sticking out of the water.

When I felt sand under my body, I was suddenly in a world of immense wonder; each detail was brilliant, almost luminous in its vivid intensity. A fly set down on my face and marched in exploration of my nose.

After a few minutes of lying with the blades of grass and the grains of sand, I heard the sound of running footsteps. I looked up to the safety instructors pounding along the shore to rescue me.

"Are you all right?" they shouted.

I croaked, "Yeah...I'm all right."

They picked me up. "Let's get you back to camp," one of them said.

Two days now, still not sleeping much even with all the hard physical work of the Outward Bound day.

This night on earth is hot and steamy. Out where I look, in space, it feels empty and cold and vaguely hostile, like it mocks all the efforts of doing good and right that happen down here on earth.

There is a feeling of intense claustrophobia. Discomfort and meaninglessness put pressure on me.

Like in the river, I don't see any way out. I finally give up. I say to myself, "I will just lay here and take whatever it is that comes. I can't get out, and I won't even try any more."

In the early morning, I woke again to the sounds of the camp stirring. I could see the sunlight streaming down through the forest leaves and smell the smoke of a fire burning. I lay peacefully still for another moment, still bathing in the rest that came through the surrender in the night. Then I heard people calling my name, and knew that it was time to join in. As I got up and dressed I realized that my life is never going to be the same again. I needed to find something that fills the hole that had opened up. I wondered what would do it and where that would be. I didn't have a clue.

I was 23 years old. Going to Law School didn't make sense any more. Going to India did. I didn't want to build another world that would just fall apart again. I wanted something more real under me. I wanted to be ready for the next journey into open space, whenever that might be.

Self and Space

When we don't understand Space, it feels like a foreign, hostile element. Space doesn't touch us like the water; it is not warm like fire. It is definitely not as personal as either. It is bigger than us, beyond us, and one can realistically wonder if it either cares about us at all or even knows that we exist.

In water and fire we still have an "other" who can tell us who we are and give us something that we can react against. In Space this other is vast, open, and, to the best of my reckoning, not very responsive to our personal efforts to manipulate it.

It just is. And the way it just is brings us back to our self.

As we come to look inside with the friend's eyes, the self opens up and reveals her secrets.

To the degree that we can take it, we realize that one of the secrets of the self is that there isn't that much solidity there. The self feels real, acts real, keeps us company day and night, organizes our whole life, tells us all we need to know about good and bad, who we should be and shouldn't be...but...in many ways it is like the little man pretending to be the Wizard of Oz. What seems like a lot of huff and puff really turns into a very small somebody when we get behind the curtains of illusion.

When we explore the self heartfully, we find a lot of ideas, a lot of old emotions, a lot of assumptions about who we are, and...a lot of open space. The self that we feel to be so real is a not such a solid thing. It is a system of illusion, something like a movie that appears as a continuous flow simply because the images come by at a fast speed.

This self is made of images that protect us, guide us, locate us, and give us our orientation to life. Our images of self are something like little computer programs that tell the computer how to run. They tend to run unconsciously, in the background of all our daily activity. The more we rely on them, the more they run us, the more real they feel.

At first we don't want to know about the Space quality inside us because that means there are holes in our defense system. Holes in the defense system feel unsafe. These holes are places where our self control mechanisms are not so efficient. We fear that we could be attacked in these holes or that something of our own inner aggressions could shoot through. With introspection, we find little ones at first.

For many people, these first holes come through relaxing bodywork where the skill of the therapist is so good that we relax out of our known tension systems. This is very pleasant at first, but somewhat unsettling to a psyche that is not ready for it.

As we continue deeper into self-observation, then bigger holes in our defense system show up also. In expressive therapies like bio-energetics or encounter, we get into places where our ego system just simply doesn't know how to cope any more. Alternatively, in some of the deeper forms of bodywork — things like acupuncture or energy work or psychic massage — we find ourselves in deep and flowing places that don't fit with our maintained personality systems. In the course of meditation retreats lasting longer than five days, we start to also come unglued.

We cannot help but notice that we are not solid, and that we have huge inconsistencies in our psychological armor. If we don't know what is happening here, this is literally terrifying. Living in an armored self has taught us to feel small and insecure and threatened by an Other that we can't control. Then to suddenly feel that our defense system against this Other has holes in it brings awful feelings. This experience is Hell when you don't understand it. Just imagine how a turtle will feel when it realizes that its shell has some extra holes in it.

Solidity and continuity are two of the core elements of our defense system. These things give us the feeling of being real and in some kind of control of our lives. In space, our personal sense of solidity and continuity find no confirmation. It just isn't there.

Because of these threats to our childhood safety system, Space remains alien to most of us. When we contract to Space, Space doesn't reveal much to us. Like everything else inside our self, Space appears in its demonic forms when we contract against it. It appears Empty. Void. Arid. Cold. Foreign. Dark. Meaningless.

Hostile to the self that is looking for subject-object confirmation. The gift of space—a unity of consciousness, a reunion with our whole self—appears as a threat.

So, as long as we are in contraction and protection mode, we will never know what Space or Self really are. We just project out on both and make guesses.

As a meditator and therapist, I am continually exploring the play of Self and Space. I know people don't heal without a living connection to Space. The self who is separate from Space is not a very real self, and its victories are essentially hollow.

This little "me" is about as stable and healthy as a helicopter in the sky. It will stay up there as long as it can consume a huge amount of energy, but when that energy is gone, falling happens. We hit the ground. The created self is very wary of Space. It doesn't rest easy in open space. I also know that Space can be extremely generous when we know how to open to it.

Identitification

The desire to encounter Space brings us face to face with the reality of our Identity. In Ice, our identity is a hard and protected thing. In Water, it is a fluid, evolving state of consciousness. In Fire, our identity is the Presence that is born out of intensity and clarity. In Space we realize that True Nature is our real identity, and we hardly know what that is.

Instead of True Nature, all we have really known is the process of identification.

In the friend's way, we realize that we create identities, and each of these identities is part of our protection system. Some identities protect us from outside intrusion while others protect us from inner criticism.

This process of identification is a safety mechanism. It is one of nature's finest safety systems. We learn to create identities in the early years when we feel small and helpless and under a lot of pressures we don't understand. We learn to create a new self where we are safer, and split away from the painful or awkward experiences of the original self.

In such times of trouble, safety comes when we discover the art of creating a new self. The new self stands outside the difficulties we are in. So, after we create it, we then identify with it...we claim it to be our new reality. Like magic, suddenly we have transported our selves into safety. This is a simple, brilliant strategy. No matter what the challenge is, we can always create an imaginary me that will somehow cope with the situation. Some of these imaginary me pieces are brave, some are cowards, some are smart, some are dull...they come in many shapes, sizes, and colors. Whatever works, we keep it and then use it again and again through the rest of our lives. All we have to do is remember this created self, identify with it, and let it run its program for our safety.

The safety system of identification works its wonders, but it does come with a price. Identities are easy to create and slip in, but they can be very sticky to get out of. When we are not aware of them as safety mechanisms, then we fight for the right to stay in them. We protect them at all cost. They are to us what a shell is to a turtle.

By staying in identities, we come to live within tight psychological and emotional borders. What's outside we want to keep outside; what's inside we want to keep under control. Every time we use our identity creating system, it takes us into escaping our present self.

As we do perform such a magic escape, we confirm the original self as someone who needs escaping. We confirm that deep inside we are deficient and in need of a rescue. Even if we think we are creating a good self, or the right self, whatever self we adapt still remains in adversarial relationship to what is outside it. The process of identification with any self takes us into an experience of being separate and threatened by something bigger than us. Clinging to identity keeps us in this kind of prison. We live as a little me, whose efforts to make "My will be done" are threatened by the bigger world around.

We know well how it feels to be in a tight, identified sense of self. This kind of self creates the illusion of being real, known, secure, and under our control. We become familiar with the feel of these contracted selves. They are our social tools for protection and assimilation into the family and world. We are so accustomed to these creations that soon we cannot imagine what it is to live without them.

Sensing this quality of danger in living inside the limited self, we tend to contract even more. We try to seal off any place where danger can get in. We try to make the illusion of the self appear more solid, more real. We do what that self tells us to do. We stay busy. We don't look inside very deeply or very often. We hope that our protection system is really good, and we are deeply scared when we find that it is not as real as we would like it to be.

In the Friend's way, we come to realize that there is something problematic in the very nature of how we create and identify with a homemade identity. The process of living in a fabricated self created in the stress of childhood is missing something profound.

This doesn't mean that these created selves are bad or wrong. What it does mean is that our skills in creating artificial selves leave us feeling isolated from the real world around us and separated from the truth of our inner being. The artificial selves don't have within them the capacity to bring true peace or true love. Realizing this, we start looking for a clearer expression of the reality inside us. We want a deeper ground of being; even if it feels less safe than hiding in the imaginary selves we can create.

Projections

Whenever we create an identity inside, we also create a shadow. We create a something which is not that identity also. Whenever we make a good self, whatever is left over becomes a "bad" self.

When we create a "right" identity, the rest of us becomes less than right, or often "wrong." In the learning to be a "good" and "right" kind of person, we create a shadow self, and we empower the good self to suppress the chaotic forces of the shadow self. That's what identity does. It splits us. It encourages tension between the good side of the split self and the shadow. And vice versa.

From the point of view of identity, Space is where the shadow lives. It is the home of all those things that we don't have under control. For the identity self, Space is as likely to be full of monsters as the Atlantic Ocean was suspected of being full of Sea Dragons in the Middle Ages. Like the Ocean, Space is a vast field where our innermost projections run rampant.

The releasing of Ego defenses and the opening into Space can be very frightening, even for the most mature individuals. At least until you get the knack of it. Each time we let go of our psyche's structures, we can feel helpless, lost, useless, small, like falling, worthless, disoriented and more. This is so scary that nobody in their right mind would do it without a very good support field. For an identity, it truly feels like dying, and we need some very clear reassurance that it will be OK or we just won't go there.

Both therapy and meditation are established ways to practice releasing contraction and discovering space. We can have support in releasing the identity patterns we are holding to. We can also realize that these identity patterns are likely to be protectors whose job it is to protect us from some very uncomfortable feelings. These uncomfortable feelings are bound to arise when the protection of the cramp and identity is released.

Be-Friending Space: The Opening

In the Friend's way, the way to know Space is to open to it, to feel it and participate with it heartfully. As with every other aspect of our inner world, if we are friends with our space, it will be friends with us. And, like everything else inside us, it takes some skill and practice to relate positively our own inner space. We need to understand that space and identity are not compatible, and that identity is a protection from the shadowy parts of our self. Meeting space means we will be open to the shadow self.

In the space element, the key is not reacting. Even to the shadow self. The ability to rest in the View and the Warm eyes allow us to see what space brings us without reacting. Not reacting to the shadow self allows us to go out of the protective identities that we have been living in. The shadow self seems awful, and will surely be entertaining as it displays again all the reasons why we wanted to make it a shadow self in the first place. We will experience or witness some challenging feelings. Not reacting to these challenging feelings take considerable trust and/or maturity, but this is the key to dropping out of the created self and into the open field of the real self.

Once we are out of our little identity shells, then we can make contact with Space again. Get the feel of it. In the Friend work, we learn to be personal with Space. We build on the lessons we have learned through Ice, Water and Fire to encounter the Space dimension of consciousness. We have found ways to de-fuse the inner tensions which project out into space.

We have developed the sense of self which can stand in an open field and know our goodness. We have recovered the fire eyes that can see, and see without being overwhelmed in reaction. In other words, we have prepared for a witnessing consciousness, the kind of consciousness which is unafraid of the reunion that Space will bring us. In these ways, we learn to court space, to invite it to unfold in our lives.

The consciousness in Space responds poorly to aggression, but to clear and heartful intention, it responds often and magnificently. We learn that we can drop into the field of unified consciousness and be given information. We can also drop into the field and take a bath in the state of being where there is no particular identity and all its struggles. We taste the deep, dark Peace quality of space.

The Unified Field

When we are able to be intimate with space, we discover its gifts.

When meditation or therapy drops us out of the familiar sense of self and into a field of bigger consciousness, we realize that this quality of consciousness is very different from the kind of consciousness we know from living inside a self.

The consciousness that lives in Space has a different program than the consciousness that lives inside a self. The pure consciousness that lives in Space is unified consciousness. It knows the truth of Unity. It allows divisions to come out of a field of unity, but even then they are all connected within this field of unity.

What that means is that Space will bring back whatever we have separated from. It will show us all the things that we have pushed into the unconscious. It will bring the bad and the good together in the same place and not favor either.

We are used to knowing our self as a good self who is managing all the less good ones. Space puts them all on equal footing. It doesn't co-operate with our child games of good and bad boy. It takes us out of that self into the Self which is bigger, and richer, than both. For the self that is split, this is terrifying. It means facing the things we have shoved into the basement of our unconscious. Anger, fear, sadness, revenge…all the things that we have pushed away will return. How could it be otherwise? How could a split self merge into open consciousness and leave parts of itself behind?

The Psychology of Space

If we allow ourselves to stay present in Space, it turns into Spaciousness. Space that is not resisted brings a coolness, an essential sense of sanity to whatever it contacts. Said another way, Space is the portal through which our essential sanity returns. We lose identity and recover our basic intelligence. In this cool sanity, the demons of rejected self that appear out of space will not be so frightening. In fact, they turn into angels. Sadness becomes tenderness, anger becomes strength, fear becomes sensitivity, grief becomes caring…

Each of the rejected demons brings with it a gift when it returns to the unity of our consciousness. These gifts are precious jewels, ways of being and relating that we had lost contact with. The sense of opening becomes very exciting as we realize any time we are witnessing and present, some new aspect of our consciousness will show up and bring its gifts.

The sanity that returns through space is the self that has no history, the self that has no story. It is the intelligence that lives in the timeless dimension of Space inside us. This intelligence manifests as Presence. In the Zen tradition this is "The face you had before your parents were born."

When we open to Space, this opening is the invitation for the consciousness inside our Field to activate.

This activation is very exciting and highly precise. Whereas the personality shell operates from memory and protection, the intelligence of our Being, the intelligence that we call out of the Field of our Space, is a precise, in-the-moment response to what is here and now.

Like the flash of open seeing, we have the ability to flash open intelligence. Our consciousness will respond to what is here and now with its intrinsic love and truth. It doesn't need all the buffers and protection systems that our personality defenses require. The in-the-moment expression of consciousness that comes through open space brings the clear voice, the clear eyes, and the clear heart that express most accurately our True Nature.

Exploring Space Safely

The easiest, safest, beginning way to explore Space is through the felt sense of the body. Feeling our way into Space is much more grounded than thinking our way into Space. With the felt sense of the body as a reference, we can sense into the boundary of self and Space. From the safety of our own feeling sense, we can explore the interaction between our body-mind and Space. Exploring in this way we generally find Space clarifying to the mental-emotional bodies. It actively nourishes our consciousness. Space universally brings good news into the body-mind when we are present to it.

When we bring attention to the felt sense of our body-mind, we can find space in two places. The first is outside and around us, at the boundary of our sense of self. This way begins with a felt sense of the size and shape of whatever experience we are in.

All of our experiences—joy, sorrow, smiling, anger—have a size and shape to them. We can easily find these patterns when we allow ourselves to relax and expand our awareness of how it is to be inside them. Whatever we are "in" will have its limits.

By expanding our awareness to the border of the experience we are in, we become aware of the bigger space around it. Feeling our way along, we can come into the boundary place and sense the contact of Space with that boundary. Often there is a negotiation, or communication, going on in that boundary place. Paying attention to this communication will allow us to release from the boundary and experience the space around the bound-aries. It is very simple and very freeing to do this, and puts whatever experience we are "in" into a new perspective.

A second way we find space is to be aware inside a felt experience. Staying present with our awareness to any body-mind experience will begin a process of clarification where the space aspect reveals itself. The key here is to feel the experience, and then to explore that experience with the flash of open seeing. In the feeling of an experience, the experience becomes less foreign to us, it becomes something we can know. In that knowing comes a relaxation.

We don't have to be afraid of this experience and we don't have to separate away from it. By looking into it with open seeing, we can examine it and discover that each time we relax, the sense of self we are in will reveal more of itself to us. For example, if we say we are angry, then we feel this anger in the body, and we look at it again, we will likely find that the initial anger has changed into something else. Often in my practice it dissolves into hurt. The real, solid sense of experience opens into a more fluid sense of experience.

With heartful attention, everything changes. Just like the Zen Bull could follow the watercourse way down from the stream to the River, and from the River to Home, we learn to simply stay present with our experience as in unfolds. In the unfolding, we discover an innate pull towards love. We also find the Space element grows.

Gap

When we are more relaxed with the felt sense of Space, then we can open into psychological Space also. For this, we explore Gaps. There are Big Ones—like letting go of an identity that we have formed over a period of time—and there are little ones—like getting wet in the shower and just being there without any thought of the day ahead or behind. In such gaps we are simply in-between. We are not attached to something outside us which gives us the reference point of who we are. We just are here with our natural senses and a relaxed mind.

The created self does anything it can to give us a safe, secure feeling of solidity and continuity. A big part of its protection plan is to defend against open space. It tries to protect against Space by contraction, mental busyness, emotional confusion, hardness, systems of denial...and more. It is usually very good with this self-generated sense of security. Even so, there is always something missing, some place where there is a Gap in the system. As poets have noted, it is through the Gaps in our ever so serious sense of self that the light comes through. A Gap is an open place in the identity system where light can come through.

In such Gaps, we find the Space quality. At first, it seems we have to break down in order to feel a Gap, but later on we learn to go looking for them. Instead of having identities taken away from us, we learn to surrender them. In meditation training, we learn to appreciate the discovering of gaps and the ability to hang out in them for longer periods of time.

One of the key ways we know we are in a meditative Gap is that the sense of time falls away. In deep meditation, we let go of many other reference points (past, future, age) that we use to keep our identity system in place.

In the therapy world, we learn to challenge the boundaries of our created sense of self. We question it, we hold it, we examine it, we allow it to move...sometimes we even allow our created self to fail, and in that failing we find the Gaps again. The Gaps come either through break through with emotional experience or with break downs of our control system. We release out of who we are trying to be and fall into who we really are.

Again, we surrender control, even if that means facing the shadow self again. With a little supportive presence, we can slide through the fear quality in such times, and find very creative ways to communicate with what is deeper inside us. We discover a new sense of ground.

A simple way to explore Gaps is through breath awareness. With every outbreath, there is a gap before the inbreath. In that gap is the opportunity to let go of what was, and who I was, and to discover what is and to open the way for this what is to unfold into a new pattern.

Navigating into the Gaps is fundamentally feminine. It is the art that Buddha sought in training his monks with the open hands and begging bowl. To go into the Gaps we go by asking. We go with deep respect in this asking. Non aggression is the key. In other words, we have to surrender the striving of the created self—getting better, getting bigger, getting ahead, getting somewhere we want to be—and surrender into a receptivity to what the intelligence in the open space will reveal today. Again, practice with being intimate with our experience will give us the ability to come into the Gap places without a sense of carrying some preconceived agenda. Another expression of this way of approaching Gaps is in the prayer, "Thy kingdom come, Thy will be done."

We ask. We are willing to wait. We find delight in being surprised by the words that form through us and the depth that opens to our heart. In this kind of vulnerability, an intimacy grows, and this intimacy is deeply rewarded by the intelligence that lives within open Space.

We find that the end of old identity patterns is not the end of the world. In fact, it is where we discover the bigger consciousness that is in Space.

As we venture in and out of the Space, as we learn to let it manifest through us, we find a deep sense of being home again. We are in touch with something precious, and that something precious is happy to manifest in our lives, to re-connect us with Being.

Having Space in our life doesn't mean that we are 'spaced out.' Real Space brings an open, fresh quality into the way we are here. We allow our selves to be in the same play of creation and dis-creation that the rest of the universe lives in. We have space for others, we have space for our selves. We lose aggressiveness and rest in the ride of the Bull.

Once again, mountains are mountains and rivers are rivers.

Earth, Water, Fire, Space: The Sequence

In the Tibetan Buddhist tradition, the sequence of earth, water, fire, and space is an archetypal pattern of self-knowledge. Each stage of this journey brings us into deeper aspects of our True Nature. It comes as we dissolve out of the identifications we have accumulated, and in that dissolving recover our original being.

In the language of the Friend, we can say it this way: when we learn how to explore our experience, we find that the world of appearances (earth) dissolves into the world of feelings (water). When we can be with feelings, we discover awareness, the fire element. As awareness becomes sharper, we realize the space quality, the openness of our selves and the world around us.

Originally this sequence was outlined as the stages a soul goes through as it separates from the body at the end of life. It may be that way, but I don't really know.

What I have found is that this sequence happens frequently in therapy practice and in daily living. It is a fractal-like pattern that in its smallest phase can happen in moments of introspection, and in its largest phase can reflect months or even years of self development.

The beauty of this system is that it teaches a clear, well-travelled path for moving inwards. It gives us the skills to discover the deeper, finer qualities of our being. We literally go from ignorance to awakening, from living in fear of our inner world to befriending it.

Earlier in the book, we said that our inner world has its architecture. In this architecture there are borders, divisions, and doors. The Tibetan sequence of elements provides a good framework for such inner architecture. Each element has its function and its borders.

When we learn to relate properly within the element, we journey to its border. There we are introduced the next element.

When we use this system as a map, we can sense where we are, where we have come from, what comes next, and the issues we are likely to encounter in each of these stages. Further, the progression carries a built-in sense of safety in it. In each stage, we learn skills that are essential for moving deeper into the unknown self. Along the way we learn maturity, a way of being with our self that carries respect and trust.

Earth and Ice

In the Tibetan tradition, the first element is Earth. In the therapy world, that means, "being here." We learn to locate into our body, and to say "This is who I am." We bring attention to the solid sense of self we carry. We get real with the felt sense of our body. We recognize our limits. We accept the reality our body sense offers us.

In the Friend's Way, we have changed the word Earth to Ice. This is because the external layer in most of us is not so earthy. It is really more Frozen. I suspect that the difference between what the Tibetan teachings offer and what I experience in my therapy practice is the focus we bring. Tibetans are not very concerned with the emotional body or inner emotional world. I am. It is this inner emotional world that first appears frozen.

In the earth phase, all is normal and as it should be. However, when we look inside the people in this earth phase, we realize that this sense of normalcy is supported by a huge amount of tension and ignorance.

In the effort to appear normal—even to our selves—we have a very restrictive filtering system going on. This ego system tells us what is good and what is bad; what we should do and what we shouldn't do. It also tells us who we are.

In the frozen world, our options are limited. We are not recognizing our own ability to change, so most of our attention goes to changing the outside world. We try to make political changes or social changes or create the kind of atmosphere in the home

110

where we are not burdened. In this attitude we miss the true nature of our own consciousness and try to find happiness from something outside us.

We carry this same political impulse with our self. We identify with one part of our self and from that place we try to organize and change the other parts of our self. We create a system of reactivity to our self and learn to live within that system of reactivity.

The challenge of the earth/ice phase begins when we realize that "business as usual" is no longer an option. Something else has to happen. For many people, that something else includes a desire to look inside, to see how we are contributing to our own happiness or difficulties.

A good starting place with the earth element is in the felt sense of the body. The felt sense of the body is a living, in the moment experience of our intelligence in action. Attention to it will inevitably melt the ice we have made around our self and bring us in contact with the feelings and deeper levels of who we are.

Water

In the felt sense of our body we find another sense of self, another body. Within the Earth, we discover Water. Feeling into this body, we find energy. Emotion. A fluid sense of self. In this fluid body, the sensations of the physical body take on personality. We are sometimes feeling our self to be bigger than our physical body. Other times we are smaller. Sometimes we are older, sometimes we are younger.

In the sigh of our lungs can be sadness or relief or a simple joy. In the strength of our legs we can find enthusiasm and a will to explore. The body is full of our own unique consciousness. It is a place where our own emotional landscape waits for us. We sense the flow of consciousness that permeates all of us.

This inner world of feeling was a difficult place for a child.

However, with support and understanding, we can learn to be at home in our own body and its water.

Water takes us out of a world of hard, fixed elements and into the world where flow and stillness abide. In the therapy world this is where we explore the emotional qualities that live inside the body. Here we learn to give movement and voice to our feelings. We learn that in the exploring of them, emotions can be bridges and doors.

If we know their ways, emotions bridge us to the world around us. They help us break through old limitations and discover a rich way of truly relating with each other. At the same time, our emotions can also open doors into our inner world.

Befriending our feelings opens the way for these feelings to take us into a deep rich intimacy within our self. We find a soft, pliable quality of our consciousness. We also find the ability to let go, and rest in a flow of events. These things bring trust, rest, and kindness. We are no longer so separate from our selves. The new sense of intimacy brings delight and renewal as well as the challenges that come with being more emotionally alive. The physical body turns softer. It releases tension.

In the water, our fluid nature responds to a fluid world. We are able to follow the flow of the inner consciousness as it flows towards its deepest resting place.

Fire

At home in the Water, we discover a new quality of self: the ability to be aware even in emotion. We find a present tense awareness that allows emotion, but doesn't suffer in it. This awareness is so fully with the fact of emotion, that it isn't interested in the cause of the emotion or the rightness or wrongness of the feelings. We are both in the water and already free from it. Here the Fire phase of awareness opens.

In the Fire phase we know our self as awareness. We are someone who sees. We realize that the ability to see is a constant.

It doesn't change even when all our experiences do change. We come into a sense of self that has a radically different sense of time. Our essential awareness has not been formed through time nor has it eroded over time. It feels timeless. It knows it has a history and is likely to have a future, but in itself there is no orientation to either one.

As we rest in this new sense of time, we also realize a new sense of perspective. This new perspective isn't confined to our body's sensations or even our body's present location. Our perspective, our point of view, includes all the experiences of our body and our feelings, but is bigger and less local than either. Most of our lives we have come from a perspective of being inside the protection systems of our body-mind. We have looked out from the assumption that we are protected by our cramps and defenses, and that our awareness has served to strengthen these cramps and defenses.

In Fire's awareness our perspective isn't limited by our defenses. Here we burn off many attachments, including the idea that the watery, feeling self is our real self. We realize that we have a clear seeing capacity that is even more fundamental than our feelings. This clear seeing capacity can see things for what they are. When it burns into emotion, it recognizes that most emotion is based on previous attitudes, previous assumptions about who we are.

In the light of clear seeing, these attitudes come into question. Are they true? Are they real? Are they a manifestation of our True Nature or are they deep codes from the protection system of the remembered self? Invariably, emotion is expressed through the distortions of our protection system, and these expressions are only partially related to the truth of who we really are. In clear seeing, we can journey through the emotion into the layers that it has been protecting. We can find a new connection with our self, and we can reclaim parts of our selves that have been neglected or lost behind the protection we have put around them.

In awareness we realize that the most essential part of us has never been hurt. Our physical and emotional bodies have suffered many insults and pains, but the awareness part of us hasn't been diminished through these pains. It is still the same, perhaps even more kind for what we have gone through.

As we know the truth of our present time awareness, we realize we are fundamentally fine in the present moment. We have survived. We haven't lost anything permanent. We come to question our survival system. This survival system has been our friend and protector for our whole life.

Even so, it doesn't orient to the same truth that the aware self yearns for. We understand our protected self cannot know truth while still hiding behind its walls of protection. To be more true, more real we want to let go of the protected, emotionally reactive self. We are mature enough to see things as they are.

Space

In Space, we separate from the smaller identities what we have called "me." We have moved out of the socially formed, remembered self. We discover our consciousness operates outside the protection and limitations of our physical and emotional bodies. We are bigger than the houses we have inhabited for all of our lives, and we are ready to live in the bigger field of who we actually are.

As the attachments let go, then the clear perception of who we are in our original nature is revealed. We learn discrimination, to clearly see what is and what isn't true on a moment-to-moment basis. In that connection with moment-to-moment truth, we find warmth and wonder.

We find a vast sense of emptiness where our clear seeing capacity is at home. We realize emptiness outside of us and also emptiness inside. We know that we are not separate. We are not alone, not abandoned, not in need to prove anything for or against. Like all of the rest of Space, we already are. Our being is pure, virgin in its nature. It has no cause, no beginning, and no end. Just like a theater can host many different kinds of plays, we are the same no matter what is playing inside us. We find our self to be vast, and intimately connected with the whole Vastness around us. In this quality we discover our deepest peace and the exquisite love intelligence that lives in peace. For those who venture far enough, this love intelligence manifests as a luminosity: we know ourselves as light.

The Sequence

This sequence can happen over the course of a lifetime, over the course of several years, and can also unfold in an hour's therapy session. It arises every time we are ready to release out of an identity pattern that is fixed and move into present tense awareness.

In the present tense awareness, we are pulled naturally into being true and real. As we follow the gravity towards what is more true and real, we leave go of previous identity patterns that we had assumed to be true. We flow from the known into the unknown, and in this flow gather confidence in our unshakeable awareness. This awareness is the window of True Nature into the world.

Through this sequence we travel as others have traveled; we are part of a Path. In that path we join others who have journeyed into spiritual maturity.

In the Tibetan Book of the Dead, this sequence is how we are exposed to the brilliant light of our True Nature. In the Friend's way, this sequence brings us into intimacy with our True Nature. As we come to know the inner "I", we realize that it has always been with us. In our clinging to protection, we haven't noticed it. In the gathering of identity, we have ignored it. Even so, this inner light has remained within us. As we recognize it, feed it with our attention, and even learn to merge into it, we realize the grace that has always lived inside us.

This grace has love and intelligence in it. Compassion. Forgiveness. Insight and Intuition. With this inner eye, we don't find the harsh criticism we knew from the super ego's inner judge. We find acceptance, and an open-ended curiosity.

We find our Friend.

Part Three

Experiential Training

Returning

This section presents practical ways to experience the goodness of the self.

In the experiences of the goodness within, we come into the positive spiral where we learn to trust our selves more, and in that trust we discover more of our True Nature. As we spiral deeper within, we find new eyes to look into the world, and these new eyes discover many hidden gems within us and also within the people around us.

All of the techniques in this section come from years of working with people in the context of meditation and therapy.

Basic to all of them is what I call a switch in polarity. This switch in polarity is what happens when we release the current sense of self and fall into a deeper level of our being. There is always a surrender here, a letting go. We surrender the safety of the known and we enter into the something less known. We drop out of a fixed identity pattern and fall into the element layer underneath... from ice we melt into water, from water into fire, and from fire we discover space.

When we allow a polarity shift, we return into innocence. If this innocence is allowed to be, and is greeted with friendliness, then it begins unfolding its petals and revealing its deeper nature. We discover again and again that the real riches come from the inner self once it is befriended.

In the therapy practice, we learn several important things. One is that everything inside us will change as we give it attention. How it changes and what it changes into depends on the kind of attention we give it. Negative attention will lead to negative manifestations of self, and friendly attention will lead to a heartful response from the self. If we are properly supported in meeting our difficult feelings, we find an attitude of kindness and understanding growing for our self. This kindness is an immense gift that serves us well in encountering our self in all the stages of its journeying.

In the meditation aspect of the Friend, we learn to be patient with our inner chatter. We see it as the shyness of the inner self, the kind of conversation that one has with a stranger. The inner self will not reveal any more than the outer self will allow. In the mean time, they chat with each other. When the inner self and the outer self are less uncertain about each other, then the way opens for deeper meetings, most often with the hidden emotions inside. If we have some experience with these hidden emotions from therapy practice, we can greet these with kindness and respect and understanding and they will release to that kindness and understanding. A huge amount of energy releases as we do this, and that new energy can take us deeper into the self that lives before the emotions. This is the doorway of True Nature.

The techniques in the next chapters provide support for you safely getting to know your real self again. They suggest ways to turn in, to release out of separation and to initiate the polarity shift where you find the goodness of being. They are all time tested and true.

Try one or two of them on a regular basis. Discover the polarity shifts and the new possibilities that open after. Being dedicated without being overly serious is recommended.

Start with the ones that are the easiest and most appealing to you. Go where you have the best chance of relaxation and success first.

These techniques are arranged in three traditional categories: Body, Heart, and Spiritual Aspiration. Pick the ones that are natural for you first.

Included in the practical material you will find excerpts of session and group dialogues. These excerpts are invitations to come inside the session room and be with us there.

In this place you can see how the patterns of separating play out in adult life, and also how the Friend attitude can creatively engage them. The dialogues are true records, though the names and details have been altered to protect personal privacy.

Body

In the Friend work, our body is one of our deepest, nearest, and most precious resources.

In our bodies we have the capacity to sense and to feel...to know reality through our sensing of it.

Our bodies are a storehouse of inner treasures. In the body we have rhythm, strength, organization, flow, and many more invaluable qualities. Our bodies are also imbued with a very high form of natural intelligence. This intelligence is not just a brain activity; it is best described as whole body intelligence where the internal organs and the muscles and the simple structures of the body all carry a built-in intelligence which is available to us when we know how to ask for it. Scientific studies have found brain-like intelligence in the physical heart and also in the gut. Traditional Chinese Medicine and Ayurveda find intelligence in all the organ systems.

Additionally, our bodies connect us to the physical world. In this connection we can find grounding and basic sanity. Allowing the grounding capacity of our body, we re-connect with Earth intelligence and Earth rhythms.

Felt Sense

The felt sense is how our body talks to us. When we become aware of the specific sensations in our body, and we allow ourselves to explore these sensations with an attitude of curiosity and respect, then a flow of communication begins. Our bodies respond to the respect we offer them. In exchange for our receptive attention, the body reveals more and more of what is inside it. The felt sense becomes a portal into deeper levels of intelligence.

In the felt sense, we have qualities of feeling, sensing, and listening to what our bodies are capable of saying.

As a therapist I have found the felt sense to be one of the biggest allies we all have in solving problems and also in recovering the art of trusting our selves.

In school, most of us learned to think of intelligence as something that comes from the brain. But for the finer dimensions of life, the life decisions that we make on a daily basis, engaging this whole body intelligence is preferable.

With whole body intelligence, we feel naturally grounded, supported, and relaxed. When we return to the felt sense in the body, our sensations guide us into an exquisite combination of thinking and feeling. The more present we can be with the felt sense of the body, the safer we feel. We find that we are safe and fine in this particular moment. We relax and allow the flow of felt sense experience to take us along a river ride of consciousness to the solutions we are looking for.

Accessing the felt sense and the innate body wisdom brings us to places where our mental capacities just don't go. The things we learn while we are in the felt sense of the body are lessons that will stay with us forever.

Frank came into the room quite upset.

"I am nervous and scared and I'm not getting my job done and I can't take it any more," he blurted out.

"OK," I said. "We'll get into that, but first, before we do, take a good seat in the chair and tell me about how you sense your body. Especially notice any places in your body that you feel safe and good."

He didn't like the invitation. "I don't feel my body very much at all, and the problems I have to solve aren't going to be solved by my sitting in some chair."

"That may or may not be true," I said."But as these things are so stressful and important for you, I'd like to bring in some help. Would that be OK with you? If you can come back to your body, just the way it is, here, now, in this chair, then the intelligence of your body is likely to switch on and help us with finding the answers."

"OK... but I still don't feel much of my body. The only place that really feels safe is my butt here on the chair."

"OK," I said. "That's a good start. Tell me about it."

Over the next period of time, Frank became aware of his legs, his toes, the bones in his feet, his ribs, and his breathing. Each time he did, he relaxed a little more into the chair and his tone shifted from being harassed and stressed into being more relaxed and confident.

After 20 minutes of breathing gently and sinking down into the felt sense, I asked him how he felt.

"Good," he said. Then he heard what he just said and was surprised. "How did you do that?"

"I didn't," I said. "I just helped you come back in your body and be here."

I continued, "And now that you are all here and sitting in a good way, let's look at the things you brought in with you."

"Well," he said sheepishly, "they don't feel as big as when I walked in here."

"Good," I said. "Now that they are more manageable, let's see how we can be creative with them."

Body Intelligence

Body intelligence comes in many simple forms. Just because the form is simple doesn't mean that the intelligence that opens through the body portals is not profound.

Following are my favorite forms of contacting body intelligence. These are the ones I practice in myself and offer my clients on a daily basis. Feel free to explore the ones that suit your nature and your body.

Grounding

In grounding we can clear a lot of mental and emotional debris out of the system and return to a simple clarity. By connecting our legs, feet, and lower body into the earth, we create a very powerful circuit. In that circuit is strength and support.

123

As we connect our body into the ground, we also connect our self into the larger field of earth intelligence. A simple kind of sanity returns.

Grounding in the body gives us a sense of location. We know where we are. We know when we are. Such things may sound simple, obvious even, but they are not.

When we are in our emotional states, we often revert into previous identities... a child, a young boy... and in that previous identity we are in some other place and some other time. We lose track with the fundamentals of here and now. At best, we are partially here and partially some other place and some other time.

For example, going to the airport is always a big deal for me. I'm in a hurry. I often get stressed and worried I might miss this flight. If I get lost in these feelings they will take me back into earlier times in my life when I missed a flight or even earlier times when my mother was stressed out that the whole family might miss a flight.

Coming back to my breath and my body tells me that today, here and now, there is plenty of time and that the emergencies I may fear are not connected with anything in the present, real, world. As the reality of the present situation takes hold through my grounding in it, the emotional reality tends to synchronize with the reality around it.

Locating Feeling

In the therapy setting, a new kind of sanity emerges when emotional feelings are re-connected with body experience. The simplest way to do this is to find the location in the body for whatever feeling is presenting. "Where is the fear?" "Where is the anger?" "Where is the hurt?" Anything real can be located in our belly, arms, legs, heart or other body location.

Again, while this may sound simple, it isn't. We don't have much practice with sensing our emotions as experience inside our body. As children, we learned to distance our selves from our "bad" or unacceptable emotions. We learned to disown them, to project them out of us, to deny them, or repress them, so that we no longer sense them as connected with us. When a feeling gets to a place where it is so strong that it can't be repressed, then we act it out and throw it on someone else. In any case, we don't connect with the feeling and allow it to have a home in our body. We treat it like an unwelcome invader.

Like most things we learn to do as children, we keep repeating these patterns for the next 20, 30, 40 years or more. We become so habituated to our way of doing it, that we seldom question the appropriateness of what we are doing. We react so unconsciously with our emotions that we lose our ability to feel them, to sense them, to allow them, and ultimately to discriminate the healthy impulses that are within them.

Creatively working with emotions is a challenge. It really helps to start with a physical location for our feelings. Once located, then we can explore the qualities of the emotion. There will be intensity, size, impulse, and age (the age we sense the person inside the feeling, using our felt sense). As the emotional world lands in the physical body it acquires definitive characteristics. We can then work with these located, felt energies in very simple ways that often lead to surprising results.

We are in a group room with 25 people in northern Europe. This group has been meeting regularly for several months with a team of therapists, and over this time has been encouraged to loosen up the held energies in the body and to begin to express some of the forbidden feelings inside.

It is my first day with them, so we are new with each other.

When I ask, "Anything to say?" a middle-aged woman glares at another woman in the group and says, "I am so angry with you!"

Traditionally in group therapy such a thing leads to people expressing anger back and forth and more "real" parts of the self being encouraged to come out.

On this day, however, something else wanted to happen.

I asked the woman, Hanna, "Hanna, when you feel this anger with Helene right now, how much are you in your body?"

I had seen that in her anger, she was totally fixed in her attention on Helene.

Hanna was surprised. She took a couple of breaths, and said, "Not much."

I said, "What happens if you come back to yourself now? Let the anger be what it is and give it a home in your body. How is that?"

Hanna took some more breaths. "I've never done this before," she said.

"You are doing fine, just keep with it," I said. "Feel the mattress under you, feel the floor supporting you, feel the way your breath moves in your body..."

"Well, I am shaking all over. My chest feels tight. My belly is tight. My solar plexus is so tight that it almost hurts.

"I don't like how I feel and I don't like myself when I am this way," she added.

"Just take a moment and allow this all to be here, just the way it is," I offered.

"It is very intense, and I don't like it much. I feel guilty too," she added. Then Hanna started crying.

"How old are you now in your feeling?" I asked.

"About seven," Hanna said. "I feel so wrong in being angry. I hope nobody sees me this way and that nobody finds out."

"Yes..." I said. "See what happens if you open your heart to this seven year old girl, and tell her, "I am with you now, it's ok no matter what anybody else says. It's ok now. I will hold you in my heart."

Hanna cried some more. "I am not used to anybody telling me it is ok to be angry," she said. "I am not sure even I have ever said this to myself before. It feels so strange...and somehow both unsafe and safe."

"Good," I said.

"But it's ok, now," said Hanna. "I am not afraid any more."

"Then let this anger fill your body again, and welcome it, just let it pour through your body," I replied. "Tell me what color is it now?"

"It feels red. Bright red."

"Stay with that red. It sounds very alive and very healthy. What happens if you let that red go through your whole body?"

Hanna said, "I feel strong, very strong and safe. I don't think anybody can hurt me when I am this way."

"Good," I said. "Let this red strength fill even more of your arms, legs, anywhere in the body it wants to go. Tell me what happens then."

"I feel stronger. Powerful. I also see I don't have to act like a child to get what I want from Helene. In fact, I don't feel afraid of Helene or anybody right now.

"And you know what else?" Hanna said. "I can't believe it, but I like myself now. In fact I like you...and Helene!"

Breathing

Breathing is another form of natural intelligence. In breathing we have the ability to accept and transform the mental and emotional energies that build up inside us and/or come to us from the outside.

For example, if a friend says, "I feel very sad today," we will likely be somewhat affected by our friend's feelings. If we open our breathing at that point, we will have a sympathetic or empathic feeling with our friend.

In our feeling will be recognition that we share a common ground with this friend. From this shared common ground, we can reply. Conversely, if we don't open our breathing, we are likely to go mental and either try to be helpful or analytical or distant...the kind of things that happen when we are not in a feeling contact with others. As we do breathe, we find that most feelings are not looking for solutions or analysis, they are simply looking for acceptance and understanding. Breathing gives us the ability to offer these things to our selves and to others.

There is a way of breathing called "Essence Breath"[10] which is very simple and helpful for bringing out our natural intelligence. The technique begins with a gentle in-breath, which is then held for a count of three seconds, then followed by an exhale, which is also held for three seconds. In the inhale we open to what is present in our bodies and feelings. We accept and take in and experience what is being offered. Holding it for a few seconds allows us to recognize and sense into what is there. The breathing out creates a sense of let go…we don't push the feelings or experiences out, we just simply let go. In the letting-go phase we relax our attachment to whatever it is that we are experiencing. That attachment can be either positive ("I like this") or negative ("I don't like what I'm feeling"). If we follow Essence Breath along, we learn to both embrace our experience, and to let it go and be open to discovering what our natural intelligence offers next.

With a little practice, Essence Breath is a simple resource for both feeling what the situation offers us, and also learning to not get stuck with any feeling. For that, we can use it for a few breaths whenever we like.

If we continue with Essence Breathing for a half hour or more, it will take us out of the psychological world and into the world of living essence. It becomes a meditation tool that brings us into direct experience of the living intelligence in our body. Because we come into our Being via the breath and the body, we know ourselves in a much deeper way than when we are simply having a mental experience.

For most of the past year, Jan had been coming for sessions every three weeks. Each session helped to resolve some issues, but the fundamental sense of being disconnected and unsure of himself remained.

In this day's session, we went to a room where we could do breathing and moving work for exploring the underlying feelings. I introduced Jan to "Essence Breath." This way of breathing opens the breath into a feeling, then holds this feeling with the full breath for a few seconds, and then relaxes and discharges the breath and feeling at the same time. One goes into a gap—an interval—space for a few seconds, and then comes back to another in breath opening into the felt sense that is now present.

Jan had done quite a lot of expressive emotional therapy before, so we knew the potential for breathing to take us into the kicking and shouting and crying that usually comes with other kinds of breath therapies. However, in this session, I directed Jan to stay with the rhythm of the essence breath no matter what happens: breathe in, feel what is there and hold it for a few seconds, and then release it all and experience the gap for a few seconds. The key was to stay with his rhythms and not divert out into emotional release.

Jan gave it his best. Within a few minutes his face reflected fear, then anger, then sadness, then grief, and then helplessness....and he met them all and kept the breathing going.

After 20 minutes, the emotions became less and less charged. In fact they hardly had a face or identity pattern around them any more. Instead there was a single soft, warm, strong, pulsing energy that started to come through. Jan's body had been contracting with the emotions and now was relaxing and expanding. As it did so, his inner being, his Presence, expanded out through his body. Slowly it filled the whole room.

He laughed and asked, "What's going on?"

I said, "Keep breathing. Each breath meet what is there, and hold it, and then let it go again and go into that space also."

Jan continued for another half an hour. Each breath revealed another aspect of his inner space and the being that is there: full and silent, energetic and relaxed. Fearless. Integrated. Old, almost eternal, and yet totally fresh, present moment just born.

When he came out of the breathing, his face was aglow.

"I can't believe this is me," he said.

"How does it feel?" I asked.

Jan shook his head as he searched for the words. "Big, fresh, open.... wonderful."

"And anything else?" I asked.

"Yeah," he said. "Peaceful. I don't have anything to worry about. I just feel so much love in my heart. Are you sure this is really me?"

"How about you? What would you say? Is this really you?"

"Yeah. It's me. I never thought I would feel it this way, though. Never thought it would happen with me."

BodyFlow

BodyFlow finds its roots in the inspiration of the Indian mystic Osho:

"And the most important thing will be to bring a little more femininity, a more soft heart to human beings – men and women both. A little more liquidity. You need not be like rocks: please be like water.

"Lao Tzu says that his path is that of the watercourse way – liquid, fragile, feminine, non-resisting, flowing, dynamic."[11]

"Sometimes the river flows fast. Sometimes it flows very slowly. Sometimes it falls with great speed in waterfalls from the mountains to the plains. But one thing is certain: whether slow, fast or very fast, every river reaches the ocean."[12]

BodyFlow is a simple standing meditation that you can do alone or in groups. It is a way of being relaxed and present in the body, and allowing the body to unwind into its natural movement patterns.

BodyFlow offers the opportunity to discover the natural, fluid intelligence in our bodies.[13] BodyFlow offers a way to process emotion and find our guidance. It helps us avoid the trap of going mental, and opens up our own unique, specific intelligence and the felt sense of that intelligence in action.

BodyFlow connects us to the ground, gives a sense of freedom and movement, and opens the space for our body intelligence to communicate with us. This form of body intelligence is so valuable and so easily neglected. Most of us have invested a huge amount of time (and aggression) in getting our bodies to perform to our standards. When it comes to listening back to the body and allowing it to talk, there is often fear and shyness. It takes some courage and a little practice to find the full richness of BodyFlow again.

BodyFlow sessions typically progress through four stages.

Grounding. Stand and sense the weight of your body connecting down to the ground. Sense the weight of the body being received by the ground and the return of energy that comes back up from the ground when we let down into it. Grounding can also mean bringing emotional experience back into the body, feeling it as sensation in the body that has definite location and definite patterns in it. Gently say the word, "I am here now" and feel the quality of your emotional experience in whatever place in your body it has a home.

Melting. From a place of grounding, we start letting go of any tensions we are carrying. We acknowledge the tension, and then allow it the freedom to turn into movement. This movement is often small, tentative. Being encouraging is a key. Along with the release of body tensions will come a release of emotional tension also. We will feel many things that our tensions have been protecting us from feeling. If we stay present with our breath, our grounding, and the natural movement of our body, then the emotional releasing is manageable. We can allow our physical and emotional bodies to melt into a fluid situation that is supported by grounding and breathing. Here we can let go of fixed forms and tensions and melt down into our deeper layers.

Expression. As we melt down into the deeper layers of our body/mind, we allow the expression of these deeper layers to come into movement. We melt into motion. We give the psyche of the body a chance to express through movement. For the real depth in BodyFlow, the suggestion is to not fall in love with <u>what</u> is being expressed, but to simply allow each and everything to have its place. Most of our attention stays in with the "<u>who</u>" is expressing... the source of the expression.

Celebration. Sometimes the celebration of BodyFlow is in pure silence and stillness. We come into absolute rest and balance inside our self. Other times BodyFlow lets go into dance and play and fun movement. Both are equally valid forms of celebrating the BodyFlow journey, and typically we are open to either at this time.

Addressing a Theme

While BodyFlow can be done as a simple meditative exercise on its own, sometimes it is a beautiful way to invite the body's intelligence to explore real life daily issues. Things like, "What is the nature of my difficulty with another person?"or "What is my guidance for...."

In the addressing the theme, we allow the movement of the body to take us into a place of softly flowing heart intelligence. Gently, we invite that heart intelligence to first hold that theme and embrace it. Out of that intimate contact arise flashes of insight into the theme.

The heart experience and the heart insight are allowed to flow through our body's movement. We feel the richness of our heart contact with our theme and the exciting new potentials that it offers. We move with these things.

Alex was 53 and semi-retired when he came for his first session. He said he felt uncertain about where he was in his life and what he wanted to do next.

I asked him to tell me where in the body he felt this uncertain feeling. He pointed to his chest and said, "Here."

I said, "Good, take a moment to feel that uncertain place in your chest. Be relaxed with it and look around and see if there is anything else that you notice also? For example what is happening there in your lower belly?"

He said, "In my belly there is nothing... I don't feel it at all... it's like I lost contact with it so long ago that I don't remember it..."

"OK," I said. "Let's keep scanning to see if anything else also wants to come in today. How is it in your solar plexus area?"

Alex said, "It's tight. It hurts. I don't like what I feel there."

I asked him to feel the uncertain quality in his chest and the emptiness in his belly and the tightness in his solar plexus and to tell me which of the three was most calling for attention.

He said, "The worst feeling is in the solar plexus. It is tight and just hurts."

I asked Alex to be present to the sensations in his solar plexus for a little while and discover the felt sense there.

After a few moments he said, "Effort. Just effort. I have to try hard and work hard to get anything done. I work and work and work and I'm just fed up with it. I feel angry and I don't see that anything I can do in the next 20 years is going to be any different or better."

I asked him, "Try to feel who is working so hard? How old is he?"

Alex sat still for some moments. Then in a very careful voice he said, "He's about seven years old. He's scared as hell about being in school and he doesn't know if it's going to be ok or not."

I asked him to stay present with his feeling: "What is it like to be this seven year old?"

A tear fell out of Alex's eye, and then he started crying.

I said, "Just let yourself have the tears and the tenderness of being with this young guy."

Alex cried for some time longer.

I asked him, "How is it now in your solar plexus?"

He said, "It's much easier now...like the war is over. I don't feel so tense there."

I asked him, "What do you feel there instead?"

He said, "Strong, and kind of gentle. I am amazed..."

I asked him, "And what about your chest and belly? Are they still the same?"

He smiled and said, "No. I can feel my belly is still dark, but now I know that there's somebody there. I don't know who it is yet, but I feel more ready to meet him… As for my chest, I feel full here. Like my heart just got watered. I see that I like that feeling of my heart being here, and I want that to be a big part of whatever it is that I do next."

"OK," I said. "Let's do a little exploration here. Stand up and let your body be loose and flowing. Especially your belly and heart. See what happens when you let the energy of your belly connect with your heart, and let that come out through the movement in your hands."

Alex allowed his body to go into bodyflow and his hands gradually rose from his side. They began to move in increasingly stronger expressive movement, almost like an orchestra conductor. As his hands rose higher and higher, a smile came to his face. The movements gradually grew softer and the smile wider.

"This is so new for me. I don't know that I've ever felt my body like this before," he said. "My body is actually talking to me and feeling good at the same time…"

Resting

Resting is another way of contacting body intelligence. In rest, we let go of our addiction to stress and busyness, and discover the quality of heartful intelligence that arises out of an un-occupied mind.

Resting may not seem so glamorous, especially in the western cultures infected with the mental disease of what the Tibetans call "active laziness." Active laziness is a mental busyness that often translates into the need to be constantly on the go. While it looks like a lot is going on, actually such behavior can become an addiction that prevents us from a deeper sense of contact within our selves and with others.

In present times, we are easily speeding along every day of the week, "on the go" constantly without even much notion of where we are heading. This is called laziness because we are not really doing that much of anything significant to our true self, we are just keeping the surface selves busy.

On the other hand, the kind of resting we are talking about is not the same thing as collapsing. Collapsing is what happens when the hyperactive state flips into its opposite: shutdown.

Real resting is relaxed, alert, and open to a gentle stream of feeling and information flowing. This stream of information can be from within ourselves, from within our body, or from the outside environment. In rest we just allow the flows to communicate with us.

In rest we come into a different level of tuning. Another level of intelligence is allowed to function. This new level of intelligence releases from the heart and body.

These kinds of intelligence operate in the slower speeds, the deeper wavelengths than the intelligence that comes from a hyper-stimulated brain. The heart's capacity for understanding comes from its ability to be in contact, to feel, to sense what it contacts without making a lot of noise and fuss about it. The longer the contact, the more the heart is able to sink into deeper states of rest, and in these deeper states of rest, find the truth that comes out of depth.

Clearly, this process of heartful understanding takes its time.

In rest, our body's intelligence also turns on. Our senses sharpen. We recover the Yin ability to receive and absorb. We come back to a natural way of relating. When we are in the mental busyness, our bodies carry a sense of stress and emergency. When we rest, the body drops out of the emergency patterns it has been in, and recovers its ability to sense, to play, to touch, to be touched.

Even while I am working with people, resting is where I get most of my information. I don't have to actively look for the solutions to people's problems; I go into rest and the solutions will come and whisper in my ears. In resting state we can literally go online with a vast field of silent intelligence.

Resting is so simple. And yet it is also so foreign to most of us.

Most of us are addicted to tension. For good reason, too. When we are in pain, our tension protects us.

Being able to tense against pain is something that we learned to do as children. It diminishes the felt sense of external pain. For the child, or anyone who is in pain, tensing our muscles gives us a sense of power and "control." We can control what we feel. We can make bad things go away.

This works so well that we get addicted to it. We learn that if we stay in tension, then we will continue to feel protected. We feel the reality of our "self." We know we can count on what we feel. We feel that we are "in control" of something, if not everything. What we can't control, we can speed away from. We can be so busy that we simply ignore what we find inconvenient.

When we are in tension, we live inside very well established, known patterns. We know that when we are tense, we can count on a very familiar felt sense of our bodies to be there with us. And it's always better to be with the devil that you know than the one that you don't know.

Contrast that experience to being relaxed and in open space. In order to relax, we have to let go of the active controlling that we are doing.

Our felt sense of our body begins to display itself. We are sensing more, open to feeling many things that haven't been fully processed. We feel a mixture of sensations as we become softer. Flowing. Both good and something not so good. These mixed feelings are both very welcome and nourishing to us, and also somewhat scary to the one who needs to stay in control. Who knows what will happen when we are open?

For sure, for all of us, sometime, somewhere, in our past we did feel open. And equally sure, some time, somewhere in our past, that openness was violated. We got hurt. It was very painful, often both physically and emotionally. We decided then and there that we would never want such a thing to happen again. Tension in the body and mind is one of the core strategies we adopted to make sure that we would never be violated again. Through our tension we build up body armor. This body armor keeps all the bad stuff out and also keeps all our inner bad stuff from coming out to other people where it could cause trouble.

It has its logic.

Kari was a 40-year-old Norwegian woman who came to talk about her relationship.

"When we both come home from work, Lars is just not available to me any more. He's busy with the newspaper and emails and after I do dinner and the kids, there just isn't much time or energy left. I want to be wanted as a person, but I feel like I'm just another thing in his busy day."

I asked her how she felt.

Kari was quick: "Frustrated."

I asked her to feel into the experience of frustrated. To tell me what all the elements are in there.

Kari closed her eyes.

She said, "I feel tight...angry....hurt...resentful...sad."

I asked her to take a moment and feel if there was anything else in there as well.

She said, "Yes...I feel betrayed. I love Lars. For many years it was the most wonderful thing in my life to be with him. It meant more to me than anything I could imagine. I promised myself then that I would do anything it takes to make this relationship work and to see that we lived happy as long as we live. And now it's like he doesn't even care."

I asked her to feel this betrayed person and tell me how old she was.

Kari said, "Oh...she's about twenty."

I asked her, "And what is it like to be twenty year old Kari?"

She said, "Oh, it's the most wonderful thing in the world to be in love and to be wanted."

I asked her to feel how it is to be in the body of 20-year-old Kari.

There was a long pause. "I never paid much attention to that," she said. "But when I do now, I feel how determined I am to make this thing work and to do my best."

"What happens in your body when you were determined to make this thing work and do your best?"

Kari answered quickly. "Control. Tension."

"Where and how?" I asked.

"I'm controlling in my solar plexus, I'm controlling in my chest... I see that all my attention is on Lars and there is just not much of me at home with me."

Kari was quiet for a moment longer, then added, "You know, when I was young my parents didn't get along so well. It was awful being with them, and I promised myself a better life, that when I found the right man I would love him and make everything work out like it definitely didn't with my parents. It took a little sorting out, but when I found Lars, I was sure he was the one and that I could do it with him."

"And to make sure it all works out you controlled yourself with tension in the chest and in the solar plexus... When did you quit doing this with yourself?" I asked.

Kari opened her eyes and looked straight at me. "I still haven't," she said.

"So what happens with 20 years of controlling yourself and putting all your attention on him?"

"Now I see it," she said. "Of course I feel cheated. Like I gave him everything I had, and now he doesn't give me that back. And I'm still hoping that if I give him everything I've got, the relationship will work like it did when I was twenty."

"Is that true?" I asked. "Do you still want it to work like it did when you were twenty?"

"No," she said. "Of course not. Now I want to be me. I don't want to be tense, I don't want to try so hard... I don't want to be such a good girl any more."

"How does it feel to see that?" I asked.

"What a relief. I've been trying so hard to keep something going and not letting it— or me— change and grow up."

"And how does it feel to grow up?" I asked. "Take your time and just

sink into it," I added.

Kari took a few soft breaths, mostly with exhaling as she relaxed and explored.

"When I let go of the tension in my chest and belly, I feel like more of a woman. I feel like I am somebody. I feel real...good...an interesting person... it's almost weird to say this, but I feel now that I am an interesting woman, not just a pretty young girl who isn't so young any more."

I encouraged Kari to keep softly breathing, and fall into a wordless place.

We spent the next 10 minutes feeling the Space quality opening as the silence deepend.

Resting is easy when we are ready to be with things the way they are. Of course, in the process of being with things as they are, we have to learn how to be with things that we may not necessarily like or want.

To relate openly with things we don't like takes some practice. Our systems are trained to ignore, run from, or pulverize experiences that we don't like.

Touch Skills

In my first year of studying to be a bodywork professional I remember watching the teacher pointing to the anatomy charts of a man who had lost his skin. We saw a lot of muscles and blood vessels and such.

Everyone was taking a lot of notes for the exam, but I heard a voice inside me say, "It's OK to learn these things, but this isn't the body you are touching."

I was surprised by this, but felt the truth of it. Then I asked, "So what is it that I am touching if not the muscles and nerves and lymph?"

The answer came back in utter simplicity: "Inside every body, there is somebody... You are touching that person."

Nancy is a middle-aged woman who came for a session complaining of a chronic pain extending from her neck down into her left shoulder. Immediately I saw the trigger points to touch, the muscles to release, the acupoints to drain tension down the arm, and the reflex points on her abdomen and foot. The treatment pattern was clear.

However, my inner voice said, "Wait. Not too fast here."

I went into a slowed down resting state. Nancy had already been subject to many years of treatment. Maybe she was looking for something else than high quality physiotherapy. Maybe another level of depth could happen if I didn't just get busy with her.

I invited Nancy to lie on the therapy table, and relax while lying on her back. I sat at her head and put my hands to the side of her head, about three inches away on both sides. I took some breaths, mostly breathing out to support both of us settling into resting.

Then my hands just went to the back of her neck and wrapped around her head in a way that could support her head with both hands. I knew I was still waiting and resting.

Softly I asked Nancy to take a deep breath and let it out slowly.

As she exhaled, I heard a sense of sadness being released. I asked her to take another breath, and heard the same sadness again.

I asked Nancy about her sadness, and a little tear fell out of her eye. "Tell me about it," I said.

She did. For the next ten minutes I heard of her accident, her trips to the doctors, her fears that she would never get well and work again, the story of constantly recurring pain that nobody could fix.

I held her neck and occasionally offered it a little stroke while she talked.

When Nancy fell silent, I did too. I didn't say anything therapeutic. I simply held her and felt the sadness in her and the sadness that it touched in me. I took soft breaths to allow all of that a clear passage through my heart.

After some time I heard a little whisper. I heard her loneliness, how difficult it was to be met when she was in sadness.

I said, "It can be a little lonely when you are sad, no?"

Nancy cried again briefly, and the silence broadened out considerably. I rested with this. After a while the loneliness went away. She could feel someone there with her, and despair of her situation turned inside out.

Her breathing changed into a deep, relaxed rhythm. A strongly throbbing pulse started bobbing in her lower abdomen, a sign that her body was now digesting her emotion.

I stroked her shoulder for a few minutes. Then I put an infrared light on the acupuncture points on her abdomen that give pain relief to the neck and shoulders.

I asked Nancy about the pain, and she said it was nearly gone.

I asked her how she was, and she said, "I feel good. You really touched me."

Most of us are so far away from our body that we feel it like a stranger. When that stranger hurts or is sick, we tend to separate even more from our body. We are afraid of what it might do with us, how it might interfere with our plans. In that state of separation and fear, we tend to treat the body with aggression.

Especially in the medical world, we treat the body with outside aggression… the latest gizmo's and medicines and things that will make it perform the way we have decided it should perform.

In the process of treating our body with aggression, we lose contact with its intelligence. We become afraid of who and what is really in there. We put all our faith in the external forces of medicine and therapist saviors who hold out the promise of fixing our body, whether it likes it or not.

For most people, the easier path is to treat the body with chemotherapy, radiation poisoning, and surgery without ever making contact with the person inside the body and the creative intelligence of the body.

Conscious touch has a way of bringing us out of that

separation and aggression. In the "Listening Hands" form of conscious touch, we use our hands to listen to the body as well as to talk to it.[14] We set up two-way communication between our touch and the body, where what we do is based on what the body *asks* us to do.

When the body realizes that it is being respected and felt, then it awakens its own energy and joins us. In this kind of atmosphere, a deep sense of co-operation unfolds.

Conscious touch is so simple, so immediate, so to the point. Touching people and being touched brings us back to our basic nature again. Touch invites us back to the place where we were before we started separating away from our selves. It gives us a sense of contacting the self that we have separated away from. We recover contact with our body, and with the person inside that body. We realize that our separation is not as deep as we had felt it to be.

Most body workers are trained to "find it, fix it, and leave" as one colleague put it so succinctly. That kind of touch can be very therapeutic when it is practiced well, like in a dentist's chair.

However, in the "find, fix, and leave" approach the body still registers aggression. It doesn't necessarily want to be fixed according to an outside therapist's idea of how it should be. Especially when there is no communication first about how it came to be the way it is now, and how it feels in the place where it is now. Even when a therapist is very skilled, the intelligence of the body will only marginally co-operate with someone who fixes it without understanding it. Many of the deeper layers of the body hide or even actively resist well-meaning therapy that is not skilful in its communication.

Between the inner support of the person inside the body and the skills and presence of the therapist, anything can (and does!) happen.

"How did you do that?" is a question I am often asked by clients and students. "It seems like magic."

Actually, there is no magic to it. Just a willingness to be in contact with the person inside the body.

Anything can happen.

In Australia, Albert came for a bio-energetics session. He was a tall, broad shouldered man with a shaved head in the Buddhist tradition and an easy smile. He told me he had been doing Zen meditation for a few years and finding that being in his sitting practice is where he wanted to spend the rest of his days.

As I heard him talk, I wondered what would bring a Zen meditator to a therapist. I had tremendous respect for Zen practice, and had been practicing at a New York Zendo for some years myself. I was thoroughly taken by the Zen Mind, Beginner's Mind approach that was transmitted through Suzuki Roshi.

From my own experience, I knew that Zen develops a powerful deep sense of presence in the body. I also knew that it tends to be rough with some of the delicate, fragile areas of the psyche. In the effort to be free of ego, Zen encourages many westerners to disown parts of their personality systems. I knew myself how easy it was to shove away any uncomfortable feeling by saying, "It's just the ego...pay no attention."

I wondered what Albert was looking for with me. I suspected that there must be something deeply personal that he wanted to meet, something that didn't easily yield to the Zen warrior approach.

When he talked, I didn't agree or disagree. I looked into his eyes and saw that there was a furtive quality there, that he didn't really make eye contact with me. Normally I wouldn't say much about these things, but here he was coming for a session to a bio-energetic therapist who (in those days) was known for emotional release work, so I decided to test him a little bit.

I put my hand on his chest and brought his attention to the area around his heart. I felt the contraction there. His heart wanted to be touched, but was also afraid of it. To my touch, the heart skittered away like a dog that has been beaten before and is shy about being offered food from someone new.

I said, "Your face is always smiling, but there's something else going on in here. It feels to me like you are covering up something, still hiding...and that you've done that most of your life."

Needless to say, he was shocked that I didn't go for his "good guy" approach.

I said, "Feel your chest right now... your face smiles but the heart hides and you're not being very straight with what is really inside."

His smile started to crack. I could feel the control around his heart also lessened. It was like the heart was happy to be recognized...even in its hiding quality which was protected by his big smile.

I forget what was said next, but I will never forget the sudden attack.

Albert exploded from his pillow and stood over me with both fists raised.

"I could just crush you right now," he said.

I felt like a rock climber about 500 meters above the ground... I needed to be fearless or I was in a lot of trouble!

I held his eyes. The fearless part came in: "Stay here...feel it!"

His anger exploded into shaking all over his body.

I said, "Stay with my eyes. Meet me. See me. Feel it."

He looked at me with intense rage for a few seconds, then burst into tears, and started shaking. He released into sadness and slumped to the ground.

I moved close him, and took his head in my hands. I stroked his head gently. He sobbed intensely.

"It has been a lonely time..." I said softly.

He put his arm around my back and cried some more. "Yes," he said. "Yes."

I said, "And a long time, too... I'm glad you are here now... Welcome."

For some time, he stayed with his head in my lap while telling me the story of how he had always been afraid of his anger and done everything he could to keep it under control and hidden. He said his father used to drink a lot and then hit people. Albert knew he had some of the same thing inside him, but when he saw what his father had done,

Albert had promised himself that he would never let this piece of himself come out with anyone.

As Albert talked, his body softened and he relaxed into a quiet, deep intimacy. He told his story and was open about the good and bad inside himself. As he recognized them both, I encouraged him to simply breathe with the feeling of it, and let go into the next. He fell deeper and deeper into his Zen meditation space, and I went with him. A deep quiet was in both of us and I let the time go and just rested in the breathing and touch.

As the session finished, Albert said this was the first time that he had ever found his inner peace while he was with someone else. He had always thought he had to be alone and away from other people to meditate or to just be himself.

I felt touched by his openness and simplicity. He was no longer hiding anything, and yet gentle as only a giant can be.

I asked him to reflect back on the session. "What happened?"

He said, "First you touched me. I don't think anybody has done it the way you did just now. I couldn't believe that you were challenging me and touching me at the same time. My body suddenly wanted to explode."

I asked him, "You know you could have hit me then. But you didn't. Do you know why?"

He said, "You kept contact with me, you held me with your eyes. I couldn't look at you and hit you at the same time."

"I know," I said. "I trusted you wouldn't hurt me if you really saw me with you."

Albert said, "You really trusted me."

"Yes, I did...and now you can trust yourself. You will never hurt anyone if you keep contact with them. I can see that in your eyes, too."

His smile lit up the room. It lingered with me for many days afterward.

Albert's story is more dramatic than most, but it shows the power of touch to bring us back to ourselves, even when the separation is very strong.

More often, touch guides us out of tension and into a deep sense of relaxation within. In that relaxation, listening hands can evoke a sense of awakening in our body. We gradually recover contact with who is inside our bodies. As we come to be at home with the who that is inside, the felt sense of the body opens.

We come to live in the exquisite mandala of our body. We experience a play of sensation, rest, and energy, a sense of being at home in our self.

Body Section Summary

In this section we have shown how the natural wisdom in our bodies can be an ally for coming into the truth inside. Grounding helps us realize that we can face a wide variety of experiences. Breathing gives us a practical, moment-to-moment way of metabolizing experience, a way of absorbing and converting our experience out of negative patterns and into positive ones.

Bodyflow invites us out of tension and into the experience of flowing with the natural energy and intelligence of our body. Like breathing, Bodyflow gives us a simple, profound way of realizing we can absorb and transform our experience.

When we can meet, and metabolize our experience, then the way opens into a state of resting. In resting we relax control, we let go of the push for mental busyness. We slow down and allow the heart's rhythms to explore our experience. We allow the understanding that comes from the heart's ability to feel and the rich play of sensing that comes from our body.

Heart Skills

The core of the Friend's way is our ability to be present with our own experience. Being with our inner flow of sensation, thoughts, and feelings, takes us into contact with our deeper self. Through such journeys we are able to release our ideas of who we should be and settle into the discovery of who we actually are.

For such journeying the heart is essential. In order to really be open and creative with our experience, it takes heart. As the song would say, "Miles and miles and miles of heart."

The way inside leads into the Pain body, through the swamps of boredom, through the fires of passion, through approval and accusation, through relationship, through success and failure, through the sands of aloneness... and finally into the soft, tender intimacy of our heart.

All in all, inner journeys are not always easy journeys. At some points all of us have our doubts, but in the commitment to the journeying, the heart finds its glow again. When we go looking for our own heart, our heart comes looking for us as well. To the one who is searching, the heart brings its gifts of forgiveness and tenderness.

This soft and tender quality of the heart is as valuable as any treasure one can find. It works wonders.

If we can get there...

Joseph and his brother were fighting again. According to Joseph, they felt connected and close like brothers should be, but they had always been different and had been fighting since as long as he could remember.

In the session Joseph said, "After that last email with my brother, I never want to talk with him again."

I asked him how he felt.

Joseph answered, "Hurt. Angry. Sad. Betrayed...all of those. And for very good reasons too."

"So you don't want to talk with him again," I said. "Is that real or does that sound like punishment?"

Joseph looked surprised. "I guess you would say it's punishment... yeah, I want to hurt him back for hurting me the way he did."

I asked him, "How long have both of you been doing that to each other?"

Joseph said, "50 years plus a few lifetimes."

I asked him, "What would happen if you opened your heart to him this time? Instead of fighting and cutting off and taking revenge, you just tell him what happens in your heart and what it is that your heart is really looking for with him?"

Joseph said, "You know, if I think of all the things in the world that could happen, what you just said would probably be at the bottom of my list of things to try."

"Up to you," I said. "You can cut off and go into isolation if you think that is going to get you what you really want with him."

"Of course not," Joseph said. "If I opened my heart with my brother I would tell him how hurt I felt and also how much I wanted to reconnect with him and how much he has always meant to me as a brother. I'm amazed, but it never even occurred to me to tell him about my heart's story."

Two weeks later Joseph came in the office with a smile on his face.

"I told him," he said. "And you won't believe what happened next. An hour after I sent him the email he sent me an email back offering to buy me an air ticket to come visit him and his family."

The heart thrives on contact... its ability to sense, know, and transform.

These capacities are in all of us, but recovering them is not easy. Using them depends on actually opening and exposing the heart. While we are somewhat free to open our hearts to others, opening our hearts to ourselves and the unfolding experience of our own self is practically a lost art.

The key to understanding why this is so takes us back to

childhood again.

As a child, we didn't know much about our heart. What we did know was that our heart hurt a lot. Often. Deeply.

From very early on, we realize that if we are having unsettled emotions or pain in the heart, seldom is anyone really with us, really on "our" side. Rarely does someone hold us and ask, "What is the matter?"

More often our emotions are greeted with some very creative lectures on how to act and behave. These lectures are supported by

1) an emotional distancing by the authorities around us,
2) encouragement for us to not give in to the flow of emotions,
3) detailed lectures on why the pain we are in is our fault and remedies on how we can prevent it from happening again, and
4) suggestions as to how a truly "good" boy or girl would handle the situation.

Clearly, the message is we are doing everybody in the world a favor when we get off the feelings we are in and go back to acting "normal."

So we have tremendous incentives to push away from the experience of our own heart, and to create a personality mask that both protects our hearts and also brings us approval from others. We learn to cover our emotions so that we appear to be a good, normal kid. We learn to distance ourselves from things like pain, fear, anger, and hurt. We dissociate from these experiences quickly and frequently. We keep ourselves as occupied as possible so that there is no space for uncomfortable things to come knocking on the door. We learn to stay mentally very busy and very concerned with external things (whether our team is winning, when is the next holiday, what will the weather be this coming weekend) so that the noise of our mental machinery keeps down the kind of things that come to visit when we are silent and still.

When we practice this system for many years, we lose contact with our heart. We can barely feel our feelings before we split away from them. Almost any experience of emotion and heart— good or bad — is potentially dangerous to our control system. The control system prefers stability…actually rigidity. The dynamism of emotions threaten that rigidity.

In the splitting away from feeling, we lose contact with our heart, and our heart loses its ability to be in touch with the world around us. We don't really know what is there because we can't feel what is there. Lacking the grounding that comes from feeling our situation, we end up in a world of memory and projection. After a very brief contact with the world around us, we split away from what we actually experience and relate to our present situation as an extension of the world we have known from the past. We simply don't know what is real any more.

Sylvie told me she feels very uncreative and repressed, especially at work.

I asked her to close her eyes and imagine herself standing in the door to her office…"What do you feel in your body when you are there?"

She paused for a few moments, then said, "I see and feel it now… I feel small and helpless and insecure."

I asked her where in her body these feelings were located.

She said, "In my solar plexus, and also in my chest. My throat also feels tight."

"How old do you feel in those tight places?" I asked her, "How old are your co-workers?"

She said, "I am very young, and they are very old, they're grown-ups."

I asked her, "And what do you do when you feel very young and helpless in a world of grown-ups?"

She said, "I shrink and hope nobody will notice me. Then I try to do my job perfectly. If I am not perfect, then I am very upset with myself."

"And when you are in this situation of trying to be perfect and feeling small in a room full of big people, how do you treat yourself?" I asked her.

"Tight. Rigid. Controlling. I don't like myself very much."

"And what happens when you are tight and controlling and not liking yourself very much?" I asked her.

She smiled and said, "I get uncreative, angry, and repressed. Of course."

We enjoyed the humor of the moment, and then I asked, "Now see yourself standing in the door way of the office. Open your heart to this girl. What is it she really wants?"

Sylvie knew her answer right away. "She wants to be liked and accepted."

I asked her, "What happens when you open your heart to wanting to be liked and accepted?"

She said, "I feel shaky, I don't think I got much of that when I was a kid."

"Probably not," I said. "And now, now that you are here in your heart with yourself? How is it now?"

"Different. A little shaky still, but I don't feel so small. It really helps to see how much I want them to like me, and that I can give myself some of that acceptance first. That way they are not so big and I am not so small. I also see that I don't have to be as perfect as I thought, and that I actually want to have a little more fun there than I have been having."

Sylvie's story is hardly unusual. In it we can see that she is quickly triggered when she opens the office door. In this reactive state, she falls out of her adult self into the sense of being a younger, small person. From this remembered sense of self she walks in the door and goes to work.

The young small self carries a deep hunger for approval. It

desperately wants to know that she is OK and wanted.

When Sylvie retreats into being small again, this hunger becomes strong. She projects the need out on the people around here, who, if her office is like most, both don't have a clue what is going on, and also have little capacity to feed her the approval she wants. In Sylvie's world, this brings the experience of rejection. It stirs the pain of being a child who didn't receive the approval she craved. Sylvie naturally fights these feelings, and in that fighting, finds herself small and dependent again.

She lands in a circle of feeling that goes round and round in very predictable patterns.

The way out of this perpetual circle is to support her heart. That means first supporting her ability to feel what she experiences, and then to support her to explore these feelings without fear or judgment. Clearly it is no easy task to acknowledge feeling like a small child when walking into the office. It is even more challenging to not attack these feelings, to not be ashamed of feeling this way. However, with support, Sylvie is able to be with her self, small and all. She doesn't fight with what she finds. In the relaxed, inquisitive atmosphere of the session, her heart gradually comes out of its contraction. As it does it discovers the reality of the situation to be somewhat less threatening than the remembered self experienced.

In beginning a new contact with the reality around her, Sylvie also receives a gift from her heart: "I want to have a little more fun there..." This option breaks the circle of feeling where she had been trapped, and opens the way for a new sense of creativity to come.

Yes — The First Heart Skill

The first heart skill to learn is a simple one: Saying "Yes."

"Yes" is what turns on the functioning of our heart's intelligence. In such simple ways as acknowledging, "Yes this is so," or "Yes, this is what I feel," "Yes" brings us in contact with what we experience. It opens the doors to a positive relating where we can bring light and warmth to our experience and find what reflects back to that light and warmth.

Saying "Yes" is so important to our heart that we go to great lengths to find situations where we can say Yes. We look for people we can approve of. We go to the restaurants where we feel Yes to the service or the style or the food. We spend huge sums of money on clothes so that we can look in the mirror and say, "Yes." Even if we are too shy to give this Yes to ourselves, we still have many strategies to coax a Yes out of others. If they can approve of us, then we can drink that approval even when we don't serve the same thing to our self.

We do a lot of things to search for this Yes, but the satisfaction of the yes also slips away soon after the doing is accomplished. For most of us, the Yes is something that has to be earned. And if it is not earned, then the No lurks close behind.

The art of trusting in Yes, is a rare and precious art.

To understand why takes us back to early childhood.

We come into the world as one of the most helpless creatures on the planet. We are totally dependent on others for physical survival, and equally dependent on others for the approval our social self needs. We need to manage the others so that they provide for us, and in turn that means we need to learn to manage our self so that we can charm existence to give us what we need and want.

We become artists in being the little being that our parents want us to be.

In such a child's world, many uncomfortable feelings come to us like muggers on a dark alley. We have little or no support for feelings like fear or anger or sadness or such. When we do manifest them, our family circles react negatively. We find ourselves in trouble for feeling the way we feel. This is very upsetting. We feel our selves as the victims of many of our feelings, and do everything we can to distance and defend ourselves from them.

We find power and consolation in our ability to deny our feelings.

Further, as our self is the one who produces a lot of uncomfortable feelings, a child becomes heavily invested in the art of masking this self. We learn to cover up what really is and serve up what we should be. This masked self—looking like a good boy or girl—keeps us out of trouble and is our ticket to social acceptance. We owe it a lot for what it has done. We also take pride in our ability to create the self that we—or others—want and to deny the self that we—or others—don't want.

We become masters of the art of transforming who we are into who we should be. This is such a big hit that we do it again and again and....well, until something major happens, we just don't quit doing it.

In the Friend world, saying "Yes" opens a new way of relating with our experience and our self. We don't immediately go for how we should be, we take a little time to be with what we actually are. Instead of going immediately for the mask, we inhibit our instinct to hide our self or to try to rearrange our feelings.

We accept responsibility for being with our self, just the way he or she is. When we are feeling an emotion, good or bad, we say Yes to being with it. This Yes is our way of actively turning, facing, and experiencing our feelings.

It is a new, creative act of power. We use the power of our choice to accept and embrace our feelings. No matter what the feeling is, when we face it with this attitude of acceptance, we find a way of relating with it. In the willingness to relate with our feelings, we find that they relate with us differently.

When we say No to our feelings, we create an artificial distance between them and us. In this distancing, the feelings go dark. They gather the power that all dark and rejected things gather.

The more we reject them, the darker and more powerful they become. At the same time, when we say No to our emotions, we lose energy. There is a lot of energy in an emotion… our energy. When we split off from that energy, we have less. When we fight against it, we have even less still.

As we deny the emotion, the denied emotion gains energy, and we lose even more of our energy. We find ourselves energetically shrinking. In that state of shrinking, we feel threatened. We are not only in a difficult place, but we don't feel our self as having the resources to handle this difficult experience. In such fear and powerlessness, we easily regress back to the psyche of a child where we were also feeling small and helpless and where we had some success in handling difficult feelings by repressing our selves. In the No state the feelings are very big fellows and we sense our selves shrinking. In fact, most people come to feel very small. Helpless. Victims. And so on. We become so small and contracted because the "No" we have to our feelings also turns into a No to the person who is the source of these feelings.

In the child's world, we learned that having bad emotions meant we were a bad person. Attacking this bad person (an art that we learned) was a way of controlling him or her so that they wouldn't bring out bad feelings. Over the years, the attacks on our feelings turn into attacks on our person. We are not only saying No to the anger we feel, we are saying No to the guy who presents us this anger. We literally attack our selves, and in so doing, shrink and contract to the deepest levels of our self.

In the Yes state, we turn and relate openly with our emotions. As we do this with heart, the power of our heart switches on. The emotions don't go dark and powerful. In the heart's light, our feelings are lighter, more forgivable. In fact, the feelings come to carry the quality of a child, and we come to feel our awareness of these feelings as an adult state. As adults, we are willing to relate openly with the child sense inside without fear or aggression. The feelings become smaller and lighter, and we become bigger and more confident. We sense our selves as bigger than anything that we are feeling. Whatever we feel, the feelings are in us, and the "us" is bigger than the emotions.

From a place of acceptance, we can explore emotions in such a way that we start to find our heart again.

In a group session Lauren asked for attention to the pain in her neck.

I asked her, "Tell me what size it is, what shape it is, and what color is in there?"

Lauren felt for these things, then said, "It is about 20 cm wide, circular, black with a very rough edged outline...and, oh yes, it has an inside of deep blue."

I asked Lauren to put her attention on the blue. She did and we journeyed through the color into a sense of open space and lightness and clarity. After some time of her being in the open, blue space, I asked her, "What happens when your blue meets the black... right at the boundary of the black?"

Lauren felt into it for some moments and said, "It shrinks down in size and the black is not so intense. Also the jagged edges around the black aren't so jagged any more. More smoothed out."

I asked her about the pain.

She smiled. "It is very small and manageable now."

"Wonderful," I said. "Anything else?"

Lauren took a minute to phrase her question. "Yeah...when I went into the blue, I felt some very open and wonderful things.

"But if you had taken me first into the black, I would have felt some angry and awful things. Why didn't you let me feel these things first? Don't I have a right to them also?"

"Good question," I said. "When we went into the blue, you came into a place of acceptance and openness. From there we went to explore the black. In my opinion, if you had gone first into the black, you would have gone there with a sense of rejection. You would have gone there to get rid of the pain and get rid of the black and its jagged edges. You would have felt a "No" to your black and got into some kind of struggle

with it. In the end, you would have known your struggle, but I don't think you would have really met and understood what's in the black. To really understand what's in the black you have to go there with acceptance. Then it will talk to you."

She smiled. "The pain is almost all gone now," she said.

And here is another story of the power of "Yes."

Lisa came for help with the fear she feels whenever she tries to do the things she really wants. She said, "These days, I'm scared to take the bus, scared to make the calls I want to make...I don't know what I'm supposed to do with my life, and every time I think of something to try, I get scared again."

After some talking and exploring, Lisa revealed a trauma in her lower body that she had held since the age of five. She recognized that this old trauma still had some power over her now...that it was contributing to the fear she had about going out into the world.

We took some time for her to settle and feel supported in her heart. When the heart was stronger and more confident, I asked her to let this heart open into the feelings in her lower body. I told her that I would support her to do that, and if anything was too much that she could open her eyes and come back to being here and now with me.

Lisa closed her eyes and said, "I feel the fear...and now I feel shame...so much shame...something happened then and I promised myself I would never let such a thing happen again... I also feel how much of a secret it has been... I never tell anyone about this part of me."

With these words, Lisa cried for some minutes.

I said, "You are doing very fine. Stay here with me, and look and see if there is anything else in there... any other part that is also wanting to be felt and seen?"

Lisa came back into her breathing again. "Yes there is...I feel a big 'No'. I feel hurt and angry and I just want to say 'No!'"

I invited her to stand and shake and say "No" and feel it.

Lisa stood up and slowly let one arm tremble, then her legs started vibrating. Before long her whole body was shaking. She began punching the air with her fingers and shouting, "No!"

In the beginning the "No" was tentative, searching for its right to be allowed. Then it became more self-assured. Each "No" carried a little more confidence (and pleasure) than the ones before. She shouted "NO!" so clearly that I asked her then to come back to the shaking and see if there was anything else behind the "No."

After some minutes, she started to cry, then smile, and then she opened her eyes."I knew the fear and shame were strong, but I didn't know the anger and 'No' were so much."

"How is that for you now?"

"Scary. I feel ashamed of myself for hiding so much anger."

"I understand... but sense your body now. How does it feel in your body?"

"I feel stronger, less afraid..."

"Can you see that this 'No' carries a lot of power in it? And when you open your heart to it, can you see that this power is trying to protect you?"

"Yes...I like that!"

"Good...feel the strength of your 'No' with you now, and tell me what happens with your fear."

Lisa said. "The fear is almost gone. I feel safer now. More OK."

One more story....

We are in a bio-energetics group in Australia. There were about 75 people in this one, and the Auzzies were very enthusiastic for the emotional release work, so this group had a lot of zip going.

Jay came into the center of the circle. "I want to get out my 'No' with women," he said.

"Ok," I agreed. "Why don't you grab your pillow for hitting, and ask 20 or 30 of the women to sit in front of you?"

He did this. I could see he was really primed for hitting and shouting, and the women were primed for hitting their pillows and shouting back. It was like the climax scene in "Gunfight at the OK Corral."

Jay was already twisting and turning his pillow and hitting it on the mat in aggressive tones.

Just before it all broke loose, I said, "Jay, in a moment you and all these women are going for it, but first there are two rules that I want you to follow. First is no physical contact...nobody gets hit or hurt here, OK? Second, I want you to enjoy it. Every moment of it."

Jay's mouth fell open. "Enjoy it? But I hate them! How can I enjoy this?"

"You asked to be here, didn't you? This must be something that you are wanting, and if it's something you are wanting, and here it is that you are getting it, then why not enjoy it? Shout and scream and beat the pillow, but remember the rule is to enjoy it."

Jay was utterly surprised. So was everybody else in the room. He started banging his pillow and saying, "I hate you...I hate you," to the women. The women were crunching their pillows and making faces and throwing it back at him.

Then suddenly, he got into it. He started smiling as he said, "I hate you...I love to hate you... I love it! I love hating you!"

The girls started laughing and teasing him back. "C'mon lover boy, hate us a little more, let's see that energy!"

This was enough provocation to get another five men out to be with Jay. They all started laughing and banging and shouting..."I hate to love you, I love to hate you...Fuck you!"

In about fifteen minutes the room was a total bedlam of banging and laughing and teasing. That went on for 45 minutes or more.

Just before the break for lunch, the room quieted again.

Jay asked, "Was that a trick or was that for real?"

"How do you feel now?" I asked.

"Happy. Good. A million pounds lighter. And I feel more like a man."

"That's what I could see in you also," I agreed.

"When you came out, you weren't ready to feel your anger to the

160

women. What you were set up to feel was your resistance to your anger... the frustration of not being allowed to feel what you feel. You can bang a cushion for 100 years at women and still be angry and frustrated if you just feel the resistance to the feeling, and don't let yourself feel the real feeling. In the real feeling, the hate, you open the door to even more real feelings."

"Yeah," said Jay. "I got what you mean, especially about those more real feelings after the hate. Strange, right now I don't hate any of the women. In fact, I had a great time with them."

"And your self?" I asked. "Do you hate him still? Did you have a good time with him?"

"Yeah. Must be about lunch time, don't you think?" Jay answered.

The "Yes" of the heart sounds simple. It is. But it is not simple minded. Within that "Yes" is acceptance, an understanding that the other has a right to be and is not to be denied or fought. This acceptance also reflexes back to us. We have the right to be. We have the right to be our self, even when it doesn't look so pretty. Our fear has its right to be. Our hurt. All of the things that we normally discard have a right to be inside us.

In the stories above, the key movement is in not fighting with the things inside us which appear unlikable or even dangerous.

For Lisa, that meant allowing an expression of "No" to come up. For Jay, that meant allowing a feeling of hate to be exposed to women. For most of us, exposing these things is very embarrassing.

We don't want to be seen as the kind of person who has such feelings. Further, for the child in us, the "No" of Lisa or the hate of Jay are dangerous feelings.

In the remembered self of the child, saying something forcefully negative to a parent is a very dangerous act. Chances are it would be better for the child to suppress these feelings and only allow them out at a later time when it would be safer.

Given that most of us are engaged in fighting within our

selves and fighting a lot of the things around us also, acceptance brings a new way of participating. We allow our self to be who we are. We offer others the same. We don't use our power to try and make either of us into the person we think they should be. We respect what is already here.

For a few moments of embarrassment, we find a deeper sense of self. When we don't fight with our feeling, the heart energy inside us responds. It rises up. As it does, the sense of self shifts. We shift out of being trapped in the remembered self and find our way of relating from our present self. The adult heart surfaces and we feel a natural sense of safety and expansion that come from sensing our adult heart.

Heart Skill - Holding

Practicing with the "Yes" heart skill leads to confidence in our heart. A trust grows that we can handle our experience without separating from it or without running away from it. We can be present to how we are, just the way we are, and know that this quality of presence will—sooner or later—call out the creative adult heart within us.

The discovery of this adult heart takes us out of being trapped in the remembered self of childhood pain and projection, and brings us into contact with the present tense life where we are. This is enormously freeing, but also brings its challenges.

We feel a lot. We don't want to control so many feelings, but what do we do with them? Early on, our feelings were repressed by our childhood lessons and experiences.

Allowing the feeling to flow back in will bring back the repressed emotions as well. We don't want to control all of that feeling, but at the same time, we don't really know what to do with it either.

As children, we only have a few options with our strong feelings. We can act them out (dangerous!), we can repress them (safer, more convenient and often even rewarded) or we can sublimate them (do something good when we feel bad).

When we call out the experience of the adult heart, we find many new options available to this adult heart. The adult heart doesn't need to protect itself the way the child's heart did. We don't need to split from our own feelings so fast, or to shield our selves from the feelings of others so quickly. Further, we don't need to judge or condemn our feelings so much. We know that having bad feelings doesn't mean that we are a bad person.

In the adult heart, we come to realize that our heart has the capacity to hold our experiences. It can be big enough to hold any anger, deep enough to hold any fear, and tender enough to hold love. We can allow a wide range of experience into our heart without fearing that any of it will overwhelm it.

We come to realize that our heart has a tremendous amount of space in it. This space, like parachutes and minds, works best when it is opened. The space of the heart is very fluid. It expands and embraces whatever it contacts. The fluid space can circle around things and feel them from the front, sides, or back.

The heart's space can contact what is inside it. It can feel the truth of what is there. The qualities of heavy or light, deep or surface, real or unreal, true or more true, color, texture, depth, age, size: all are easily known in the sensing of the heart's embrace of our experience. We discover that we don't have to live in the world of remembering and projecting; we can actually be present and know what is true.

I remember standing in a long queue for the baggage security check for an international flight. I was carrying some delicate medical equipment that shouldn't be opened or roughly handled. When I saw how other passengers and their luggage were being treated, I was afraid. What if they do this with my things? The fear had time to play, and soon became an anger at the humiliation of being roughly searched by the airport security drones. A kind of hatred started to set in, and suddenly I was lost in hating the line, the people, the security system...all kinds of things.

As the line was long and the situation took its time to unfold, I took the story as a play. I let the fear and anger be, and opened to breathing with both of them. I practiced breathing in the fear, and breathing out the anger until the anger was cooler. Then I switched the other way, breathing in the anger and breathing out the fear. The feeling intensified briefly, then became more comfortable. Somehow I was now a host to both, and at the same time, bigger than either.

Then an old familiar voice said, "If I feel fear and anger here, then I bet others must also."

A smile came with that. I looked around and saw many people who were busy dealing in their own ways with the aggravation of the situation. Many people in the line looked uncomfortable and like they were covering their discomfort with an avid interest in USA Today newspapers. I also saw many of the inspectors were acting a lot tougher than they really felt. I could feel what it must be like for them at the end of their day. Sure, they put out a lot of abuse, and equally sure, they got a lot back. It was hard to tell who was the chicken and who was the egg here.

I was touched by how stressful the scene was for the human part of all of us. In that moment, I remembered the old Tibetan training for compassion.[15]

I said, "May I breathe in the fear and aggression of these people and breathe out love to all of them."

As I did so, I could feel my heart expanding to take in the stress I saw around me, and I could feel the tenderness of my heart opening as I would breathe out love.

In this simple breathing came a new perception of the situation. I saw all of us simply as people doing our jobs. I also saw that as I connected with them as people, just like me, a kind of natural friendliness arose. We were all sharing an uncomfortable situation together. With that came a natural flow of kindness, a little sense of wanting to support them in their job.

My timeless space was suddenly interrupted when I realized I was now at the head of the line. I smiled when I met my inspector and asked how he was doing this day. He was surprised, and returned the smile as he sorted through my gear. We chit chatted about travel and weather and medical equipment and he waved me through.

And when I was on the other side, I noticed that the fear was gone and a sense of warmth was lingering still.

The holding quality of the heart brings first the power to know, and then the power to transform. When we embrace something with our heart, we can know it. As we allow the heart's intelligence to know what we are feeling, then the holding of the heart becomes even more dynamic. Whatever we hold, melts. The love intelligence of the heart interacts with whatever experiences it contains. The rough jagged edges smooth out, the dark unknown (unwanted) parts of us are welcomed with light. Whatever we hold melts into something more fundamental, something more true. Anger melts into hurt...hurt melts into sadness... sadness melts into loneliness ... loneliness melts into tenderness...tenderness melts into love...love melts into forgiveness and gratefulness. And so on. Sometimes these things happen instantly; some times the changes evolve over years. The timing of the heart's work is best left in the hands of the heart itself.

While the physical totality is important, what really melts feelings faster than anything is the openness of the heart to the feeling.

First comes the holding, the being with the awkward, embarrassing protections we carry. In that being with, the protections feel respected and not fought.

As they are respected and not fought, they lose their defensive quality and gradually melt into deeper, more tender layers of the heart. When we come into these deeper layers equally respectfully, equally willing to hold them and know them, then even more trust is generated and we are slowly invited into the places where the real wounding of the heart lives. Here we have a rare opportunity to hold this wounding and be with it. If we have the maturity to be non-aggressive with this wounding, to not blame anyone for it, to be gently present there, then the transforming quality of our heart activates.

In my story of being in the queue at the airport security, noticing and holding the discomfort of my feelings began a process that took me from fear and anger to friendliness and care. I was just willing to hold these uncomfortable things, and the heart did the rest. Along the way, the support came through in the Tonglen compassion breathing where one breathes in the discomfort of others and breathes out love to them.

Beth came to see me because she was depressed. Her last relationship hadn't worked out — she found out that he was secretly interested in someone else. It threw her into such a downward spiral that she went into burnout and had to take leave from her job. She came to me for counseling and energetic re-alignment about six months later.

I asked her how she was feeling now.

Beth said, "I'm just sad about it all. Every bit."

I asked, "How does this sadness feel?"

She said, "You know, just sad. That's it."

I asked her how long she had been that way. She replied that it was over six months now.

From this brief little exchange I had already learned two things. First, that Beth wasn't really present with her sadness. She had an image of sadness but she wasn't breathing it and feeling it. Second, I suspected that Beth wasn't really just sad. The image of sadness was a protection from something deeper. Experiencing this something deeper was so scary for Beth that she was in a holding pattern with this prolonged "sadness." Said another way, the sense of feeling sad was safer for her than to open to some of the deeper feelings like being angry or lonely or in genuine despair.

I asked Beth, "How is it in your body now? What do you feel there?"

She said, "I'm tired. Tense in the shoulders, some tension here in my belly. I'm having a hard time keeping my eyes open today. I don't know why, just like I want to sleep all day long."

I could hear from what Beth was saying that she was close to the edge of what she could handle, so I directed the questions into safer areas about her past. Beth admitted that she was always trying to be a good girl, a good partner, a good employee, a good person. She couldn't understand why things didn't work out better for her when she was working so hard and doing her best. It was clear that the good girl was really struggling right now.

For Beth, being a good girl meant not recognizing her fear and anger. In such a stressful time, a good girl was allowed to be sad, but a good girl was not supposed to be hurt and angry. She was firmly caught in the child pattern of only allowing what is "good," and suppressing what is "bad." In so doing, she had also lost connection with her strength and vitality.

I asked Beth to feel in her body where the "good girl" was now. She said it seemed to be in the solar plexus where the tension was.

I asked her to lie down on the therapy table and softly breathe around the tension, just to be with it without adding any more stress. I also held her neck to offer a sense of support. With the touch support in her neck, she easily began breathing and crying came soon after.

At the end of the session, Beth found herself standing good on the ground again. She said she wasn't afraid of being herself any more.

Over the next sessions, Beth gradually found a way to tune back into the sadness by locating where it was in the body and breathing into that place. As the breathing progressed the shell of sadness fell off and the deeper feelings of anger and despair and feeling basically unwanted all of her life came to the surface. By breathing with these things she moved through each of these identities into a place where she felt her courage and her strength again. Each time she did, she felt more secure In herself, and more "on the ground."

Heart Skill - Intelligence

While many journey stories are good models for ventures into the inner world, Homer's Odyssey is a grand-daddy of stories indicating what we find on our journey Home. In the Odyssey are many rich metaphors for what we encounter when we seek to be return to True Nature. There is the open sea, dangers of all kinds, siren songs of delusion, helpful friends, fortunate breezes, storms, losing hope...finding oneself washed ashore naked. And, a beloved soul mate that dutifully weaves for pretenders during the day, and unweaves and waits for her true mate in the evening.

For the Friend's way the part of the Odyssey where Odysseus meets the Cyclops especially stands out. The Cyclops is a large, ugly, mean, human-like monster whose main feature—besides being oversized, mean, ugly, and heartless—is that he has only one eye. He traps Odysseus and his men and keeps them imprisoned in a dark cave while he proceeds to eat them one by one.

In the personal inner world, we also have such a monster as the Cyclops: our inner critic, or super ego. The inner critic is the inner voice that tells us (ad nauseam) what to do, how to do it, when we are right, when we are wrong, when we are good, when we are bad...it is the non-stop stream of inner commentary that runs in our minds.

Our inner critic is like the Cyclops in that it is big, ugly, and having only one eye (the mind's eye). Further, it tends to keep us locked in dark caves of self-rejection as it slowly eats our energy piece by piece.

In the Odyssey, Odysseus blinds the Cyclops by running a spear into its eye, thus allowing for his men to escape.

In our Friend work, we aren't so dramatic. We simply bring in the other eye—the heart's vision—to balance. The inner critic is brutal, but the vision of the heart can bring a quality of love intelligence to us that melts even the hardest, toughest cases.

When the vision of the heart joins the inner critic, we have tools to see deeply and compassionately into our selves. We are able to see how we are set up, but we don't attack our selves or make anybody wrong for it. In such clear and compassionate seeing, we are freed from the inner caves where we have been hiding from our own self-judgment.

Freeing our selves from the attacks of self-judgment is as important to our inner journeying as getting out of the Cyclops trap is for Odysseus to continue his journey home.

In many times, we will attack and judge our emotions and accompanying sense of self as they show up. Generally that's the safest thing to do. When we do, that means we simply have to be patient and take extra time in the place where we are. The inner world won't open its doors to the harshness of our inner critic. Aggression seldom elicits a soulful response, and our inner being is even less enamored with it than our surface personality.

Because the tenderness of the heart has been exposed to so much abuse, it is well defended (for good reason). First we were abused by authorities around us; then we acquire an inner authority to control us for the rest of our lives. The effects of our own attacks are more painful and strident than anything we would allow from somebody outside. A lot of the function of the therapist is to protect us from such attacks while we learn to feel our way back into our hearts.

Stacy told me she had a rough, controlling father and now she was having a hard time connecting with men. She could flirt and she enjoyed the intellectual repartee, but when relating felt as though it could become deeper, she would feel like she simply wanted to disappear.

In the first session we explored the feelings in her body through Rebalancing bodywork and Samassati Colortherapy. At the end of the session she lay on the table saying she felt very relaxed and open.

"Wow..." she said. "I get to be me again. I feel open and fresh and strangely confident."

Two weeks later she came in with a frown on her face. I asked her how she was feeling.

Stacy said, "I'm angry, and angry with you. I felt so good when I left here and then I went out and got hurt again and I felt worse than ever. I don't like this at all and wonder if any of this therapy stuff is worth it."

I felt uncomfortable with her story, especially since the last session had ended on such a high note. Often there is a "rebound" effect after groups or sessions where the highs fall back into lows and the open parts are attacked by the parts of the ego that are afraid of losing control. Such things are part of the usual growth process. Even so, I was not expecting Stacy's anger to come out so strong and so soon.

"Stacy," I said, "I'm going to respond to you in two ways. One of them is personal and one of them is professional. At the personal level I have to say 'I'm sorry.' The last thing I would want is for you or anybody else to be upset because of something that I have said or done. So from the personal side of me, a deep apology. 'I'm sorry.'

"Having said that, I must admit that the professional side of me is now really interested. I would have expected that the anger would come sooner or later, and while it is sooner than I have expected, I'm glad that it is here now and in the open."

Stacy said, "I hate being angry. I don't like it. It reminds me of being a little girl with my father again. Being angry and helpless. I hated it."

"Ok... just come back to your body now and open your breathing so that the breathing matches the energy you feel in your body."

As she did, I continued, "Tell me what happens as you allow the anger to be here without any judgment or opinion about it...just allow it to be just what it is and give it space in your body."

Stacy said, "I'm not so used to that, but I'll try...I'm breathing a little faster now and it's more in my chest. I feel hurt and angry and I don't know if I'm going to break down and cry or explode and hit you. They all feel possible."

I encouraged her to stay with the anger and let it have a place in her heart.

Stacy said, "It's getting stronger now. Red. My head wants to attack it and make it wrong, but I'm not going there now. I just feel this red stuff going through my arms and legs and filling my chest as well...My breathing is getting slower now, and I feel strong...no actually I feel very strong in my legs and arms and belly."

"Keep going," I encouraged. "What happens as you sit in that strength?"

"I feel powerful. Very powerful. I also don't feel afraid. I don't feel like a little girl any more. I am strong. Even my heart feels strong now. Wow...is this really me?"

"Stay with it." I said. "What is happening with the anger and hate?"

"I don't feel it as anger and hate."

"What do you find when your heart opens to what is here and now?"

"The anger isn't so bad any more...actually I feel she is more hurt than angry."

"And how is it to be with the hurt now?"

"Strange...." Stacy said. "In the past it was almost overwhelming. Like it could just crush me and keep me in my room for days without ever wanting to come out. Now I don't feel so put down by it. I'm strong enough to handle it in fact. I wonder why I never knew that before..."

"One last thing," I offered. "From this place where you are now, take a look at your father. What do you see there?"

"Oh, I see him as a man now, not the big Father that I knew. When I see him as a man, I see that he's hurt and angry....My God...did I just say that? He's hurt and angry...I'm hurt and angry...."

In Stacy's story we find a familiar theme: most of us don't feel safe enough to explore our experience, to allow it to unfold. We cling to an inner critic which judges what we experience. The inner critic is an important vestigial trait from childhood; it protected us and gave us a sense of orientation (right and wrong) when we didn't know what was expected of us. In childhood, the inner critic tells us what is good, and tells us who we are. When this vestigial trait continues into adulthood, it turns into a Cyclops. We are aggressive with our experience and with our self. We constantly try to reduce our adult experience into a framework that a child would say is good or bad.

In such attacking, we prevent the fluidity of consciousness from unfolding. When we experience our anger, and we quickly judge our self for this anger. Now we are not feeling the anger any more, we are feeling the judgment on it. Often we compound this separation from our self by blaming others for our experience, and turning our attention to changing them. We are caught in the struggles for and against our original experience.

In the presence field of a good therapist, many of us can easily slide past the super ego attack stations. Here we can begin to experience directly the truth of our emotions, and in so doing, find that our heart can hold them and that they will respond to this holding by opening.

In that opening, the heart's intelligence can interact with the state of feeling. We can discover the more fundamental under-standing of our anger and more fundamental truth of who we are. These naturally arise as we allow the melting of emotion and the melting of the heart holding the emotion. The process is deeply rewarding when we catch the knack of it. It is like Odysseus finding his ship again.

The more difficult part comes when we are alone again, when we are not connected into an external supportive presence field.

In such times, we can find our selves deeper out to sea than we usually venture, and again in some kind of difficulty. It takes time, maturity, understanding, and experience to not allow the inner critic to take over and attack our experience. There will be every tendency to revert to the child's response to danger, which is to attack the self and make it rigid, known, and approvable again. For Stacy this shows in her "I hate it when I am angry." This is the safety place of a child, to hate our selves for being the way we are. We gather a sense of protection this way, but the cost is that we are experiencing our judgment (hate) and not our anger any more. When we do that, the anger is not known and will never dissolve and take us on its journey into freeing our own resources. We stay stuck. Sometimes forever.

A few simple techniques can be very helpful when we are on our own with our emotion. One is to ground any feeling in the body. By grounding our feeling in the body, we discover that any real feeling has a place in the body, a location. When we sense into this place we can then feel the present tense qualities of our emotion. We can allow the breathing it wants, and also release the movement that it would like to do. The more we can be present with an emotion as an experience within our body system, and the more we can allow our body to co-operate with its breath and movement, the more we will own our emotion. As we own our emotion, it becomes less fixated on the outer triggers (people, events, things we liked or didn't like) and becomes more a quality of our self in action. Being friends with this self in action allows it to move, express, and ultimately to unfold its intelligence in some very creative ways.

Another way of working with feelings when we are on our own is to see our emotions as protection.

Anger and fear are protections for something deeper. If we judge these protectors, then we will end up fighting them or resisting them. When we fight against protections, we are likely to lose as these protection layers are pretty tough. However, if we hold them respectfully and ask, "What is under you?" or "What is inside you?" then they will respond by allowing us to go into the deeper, more vulnerable layers. In these deep and vulnerable layers we find remarkable opportunities to be more truthful and creative. Each time we are truthful in these deeper layers, a big release of heart energy comes along.

As we journey from layer to layer, there is joy in being more truthful with our selves. Further, as we go farther inside, we come into the original tenderness of the heart. And in that tenderness of the heart is our ability to flash open the heart's love intelligence. It is always a wonder how pedestrian emotions like fear, sadness, jealousy can be the catalysts to an inner journey where we find the deep intelligence of our hearts making some very creative responses to our present time reality.

When allow the heart's intelligence, we come to trust the heart's alchemy. Whatever is held in the heart's intelligence will change. And so do we.

One-eyed Cyclops is a poor substitute for the true intelligence of the heart.

Heart Skill - Discrimination

Most of us relate to our feelings like a hit and run accident: they hit us and we run. As is the case with anything that we run from, we don't really know or understand what we are actually meeting.

When the heart opens to our experience, we don't run. We stay, we feel, we expand, and we allow intimacy. We merge into one field, and in that field we can love and see clearly what our experience actually is.

In this atmosphere, the heart's intelligence switches on. In this field of love intelligence, comes a sense of knowing. We can feel and know and discriminate[16] in our experience. We are able to discern both the fine details and the broad scope of what we meet.

In an early morning's Bodyflow session, there is a group of 22 people in Sweden. We begin with each person saying a word out loud which summarizes how they feel, and then bringing their body into a position that matches their feeling. We all do this, and breathe softly with the felt experience of having our body in this position.

After a short time, I invite everyone to look inside and see if there is something deeper now, some new feeling that is just under the one above. We all say the word of this new feeling and then shift into the body position that goes with it. Again, breathing and feeling this new state is encouraged. We continue in this way for another few layers in and follow the same basic procedures.

After some time, I invite people to go into the feeling place that seems the most true. Invariably everyone stays with his or her last position.

I ask them to feel this position as a place of protection, a kind of shell. Inside that shell is something warm and tender and fluid and quite capable of moving. I ask them to open the heart to this place inside the shell and allow it to move through whatever part of the body — arm, leg, foot, hand, head, mouth — is available for moving.

Over the next 20 minutes we unwind into movement as one part of the body after another joins in the moving that comes from within.

We finished the session with lying quietly and resting in the open space that comes from freely allowed movement.

The morning exercise ended with a chance for people to share what had happened for them.

Anders said, "I came in sleepy and tired and not wanting anything but coffee. When you asked us to say a word, my first word was 'No!' I curled up on the floor and with the breathing and feeling the 'No,' it turned into a feeling of sadness. I realized then that I was still carrying a feeling of not being good enough from the day before. I curled up even tighter on the floor and held myself there and felt that and it turned into a deep sadness that I was never good enough and that took me back to being a child and feeling that no matter what I did, my parents didn't give me the feeling that I was wanted and good enough."

"And what do you do when you don't feel wanted and good enough?" I asked.

Anders said, "I push. I make myself perform. I do it right, I do it well. And if I don't get my coffee, I do it angrily, too!"

We laughed together for a few seconds. Then he continued.

"These things have been with me for the last 35 years...I didn't realize how heavy they were. When you invited us to see this last place

as a shell and to feel what is inside that shell and what wants to move there, I was surprised. It didn't feel like I was in a shell, I thought I was in my real feeling. But I tried it, and opened to the idea of something else in there.

"I remembered my heart all of a sudden. Then there was a deeper place inside, something that was saying, 'Please let me out. Please let me move.'

"I didn't know exactly what this was, but it felt like a voice that had been inside me a long time. As I let this move and unwind, my whole body started trembling. Soft at first, then stronger and stronger. Like something really important and strong was inside, but also that it had been hidden for so long that it was very shaky about coming out.

"I both wanted it and was scared of it. It really helped me to let the body keep moving and to breathe with the feelings. Otherwise I think I would have just stopped it and gone back to being normal."

"The shaking gave me a feeling for how much I was asking for love that I never seem to get. I felt so shaky in there. So raw."

"At the same time, when I let myself just shake, there was a sense of something all right in me, something like feeling myself for the first time."

"And how is it when you open your heart to this shaky raw person?" I asked.

Anders closed his eyes. He stood up and let his body softly sway. His left hand came out in a movement of gently opening to something/someone outside. He allowed this to move for a few moments, then he said, "There is an asking in me...asking 'Do you love me? Am I ok?' That asking has always been there, but now I can feel my heart behind it. I am not afraid of this asking, I am ready to stand behind it and support it. I am moving and feeling ok about myself. I never could ask and feel ok about myself at the same time before."

When we are capable of being present with our experience, we can allow the heart's intelligence to discriminate what it really is. Are we just angry or sad or hurt? Is there something more? What is that something more? What is it like to have these experiences in our heart's field in the present moment?

As we get the feel for our experience, we also get a feel for the person who is having this experience. Who is it that is having these feelings? What is he like? How big is he? How old? Is the one who feels the hurt someone who is actually hurting right now? Is he hurt at all?

If we follow the flow of the journey along, we discover that there is someone present who is not diminished by all the hurtful experiences that they have had. Some part of us is deeply wounded. And...or also... some part of us is still very fine, right now. Both are equally present and both have their truth.

Discovering the aspect of our self which is deeply hurt opens the door to discovering the one who has never been hurt. Being willing to open to the first also opens us to the possibility of discovering the second.

In Anders' story, as in many of the stories in this book, the heart's capacity to discriminate in his experience allows him to journey through the layers of remembered self and back into being the present one. Each act of discriminating awareness by the heart brings a sense of joy in being more truthful, more honest with one's self.

In this love quality, we can quickly journey through much of the difficult terrain of the heart's space: the loneliness, fear, sadness, grief, anger, hurt. In effect, we learn not to fear these places or to get into a fight with them. When we learn to be with the fear and pain and sorrow inside us these things become more open.

They are not hard, fixed memories that we are stuck with. Instead these feelings are more like open spaces, the architecture of our heart's field. We just realize that they are part of us, part of our journey, and that we can learn things through them that will make us richer if we are open to such learning. With good discrimination, we don't bump into the walls of our inner architecture, we can see where the doors are.

By relating with these emotions from the heart, we also enter into relating with the pieces of our self that have been split off in our effort to separate from these difficult feelings.

When we feel the "who" is inside a feeling, we naturally open to that person. We sense their struggle and we also sense the rejection of how they have been split off in our attempt to distance our selves from difficult or shocking experiences. We meet such members of our inner family with warmth...like someone who has been far away and is now returning home.

Heart Skill - Manifestation

When the heart's love/intelligence flows, we discover that we can relate more creatively with others and with our own experience. In that relating, we stay present to what is offered, and discover that by staying heartfully present, we are invited deeper and deeper into truth.

Sooner or later, in the unfolding of our heart, we recover a deeper sense of Being, the felt sense of basic goodness. This basic goodness is warm, confident...a good ground to stand on.

We know that our feelings and experience are not wrong or bad, and that we are not wrong or bad people for having anger and fear and such. Even the darkest thoughts have their light when we hold them. When we see how our fear transforms into sensitivity, or our hatred transforms into intelligent strength, then we develop a confidence that whatever else we meet will also, in its time, transform into something of value. We find a simple confidence that anything we meet will work out.

In this confidence we are ready to meet what comes our way. We are not defending or hiding, rather we are willing. We might win or we might lose, but we are ready to play the game. This sense of self is amazingly different from the defended, fearful self we have grown up to be. It is generous, basically concerned with sharing its love, and fearless in itself. It wants to be true to its

True Nature.

This deeper layer has the impulse of the heart.

Recall the snowflake image: each of us is unique, intricately structured beauty.

We are all a gift from the Grey Zone to planet earth. Once we realize that we are good inside, then we are free to realize our own specific goodness: If I am like a snowflake, what is the nature of my individual structure...the truth of my own self? What is my way to be here? What do I want to offer? What is my gift to planet earth?"

We want to know and manifest the impulse of our heart.

Some extra terrestrial coming to planet earth might think, "Hey, isn't it the most natural thing in the whole world to be yourself and share that with other people?"

Anybody who grew up here on planet earth would know something different.

Robert fell into his chair for the session. It was after 5pm and I knew he has a long, trying day at his banking job, but there was something more in the way he slumped into the chair than just having the 5 o'clock blues.

"I hate it," he said. "I hate this job, I hate this bank, I hate that they tell me how to run my department. I hate that they want me to fire people. I hate that they don't get back to me on the report I submitted about making our department run better. I hate the feeling of having some foreigners sitting on the board of the bank and making cuts in the jobs of people they don't even know or care about."

"Whew," I said. "That is a lot... have a look and tell me if there's anything more as well."

"I knew you were going to say that," he said. "You are always taking what I say and asking if there is anything more, and, of course, there always is... What is it today? Today I feel angry and hopeless. Why do I get out of bed for this bank? Why do I do this to myself?"

Having worked with Robert for many sessions already, I knew that he had a good intelligence and was well grounded in himself. So I tried a surprise tactic: "Robert, I can hear that you are angry and hurt and tired and that you work for a dysfunctional bank. Can you tell me what any of that has to do with you right now?"

Robert was utterly surprised. He sat up in his chair and looked at me in disbelief.

"I mean it," I said. "All of these things are real and important, but still, what do they have to do with the guy who is sitting here right now?"

Robert was confused, but he is also a fighter. "Well," he said. "I feel those things. That's what they have to do with me right now."

"Ok," I said, "I respect that you have felt these things earlier in the day and that you don't like them, but look again and see, 'What is your truth right now?'"

Robert could see that I am also a fighter, and he somehow respected that. He sat straight and took some breaths. "Right now I feel tired on the outside, but inside of that it's different. I'm not tired, and I'm aggravated, but not angry. If I stay with the aggravation I see that I'm feeling challenged and something in me likes the challenge and something hates it... like you are waking up a sleeping dog or something.

"I'm curious, curious about what is going on here. If I go inside that curiosity, I feel a mix of things, like somebody is not just listening to my story, but they are also wanting more from me. I like it and I don't. I feel exposed."

"Stay with it," I said. "I am right here with you. Keep going."

"I don't usually feel this warm. is it because you are here with me, or because I am here with myself?...or both? It's strange how alone I usually feel in this place. Somebody is being exposed and he is not sure yet if that's a good thing or not."

"Stay with it," I encouraged. "I'm here with you all the way."

"Something inside is relaxing... shaking now. I don't know if I am going to laugh or cry or both... I feel happy/sad at the same time. I'm here. Here with me. Strange, I don't think I'm doing that very often... if at all. Now here it is, and I want to laugh and cry together. You know *you have tricked me. Now that I am here with myself, I don't feel any of those things I said earlier are so real. The bank is a million miles away. And my body is tired, but I am not."*

I nodded. "Tell me about the guy who is here now?"

"I don't know if I can. I don't feel old and I don't feel young. I don't feel small, but I do feel bigger than usual. I also don't feel as heavy as I am used to... there is something lighter about me. I feel free and not particularly stuck anywhere. Strange, now there is some light and space around me as well as inside me. How did that happen? I don't know, but I like it. I feel good, even a bit playful. From the inside I can see this Robert. He is not such a serious guy as I would have people believe.

"I stay a little longer in the heart, and there is a green color in there. Spring green, a lighter shade. I feel soft and fresh (how did you do that?) and like this is a new time and a new day and that the whole world is open to me...and at the same time, I don't have to do anything."

"Ok...so stay here with this green and fresh feeling. What would it say to the guy who walked in tired and upset about a half an hour ago?"

"What would it say...what would I say? I would say to him that he's tired and angry because he's putting all his attention on the wrong things. He's struggling for a lot of things that don't mean very much. He's not really there (or is it here?) with his heart."

"And being here with your heart... How is that?"

"Sigh... I knew you were going to ask that. I feel happy, that's clear. Simple. Happy for no real reason at all. I wonder how he's going to go to the bank tomorrow."

"Maybe wear something green," I said. "Surprise yourself."

In the movement into the heart we realize that our sense of self has been built around the conviction that we need to protect our real self and to hide the many flaws we sense in that real self.

As young ones, we master the art of suppressing and covering this self. As maturing adults, we realize that our protection serves us well, but it is also a cage that traps us. We can't share ourselves and hide and protect ourselves at the same time. The new sense of self and the old sense of self have some serious negotiating to do with each other.

Sooner or later we find that releasing the love quality and creativity of our heart is what we want to do. We want to manifest our truth. When we are in our love quality, then the present moment is suddenly so full that the past pains and abuses are much less relevant. When we are creative with our present situation, then in the present moment we realize that no matter how strongly we have been hurt, no matter how lost we have felt, no matter how badly we are bent out of shape, in the present moment we still have the capacity to be our self and to share what that self has to share. In Eckhart Tolle's famous phrase, we recover "the power of Now."

Experiences in manifesting the truth of our heart are so fulfilling. We can surprise our self on a daily basis, we can offer our goodness into the world, and in the offering of it, find that there is more of it than we had ever imagined.

Heart Skill - Presence

When the natural movement of the heart is allowed, then we also discover the heart's stillness.

Allowing the natural movement of heart brings relaxation. In time, this relaxation deepens into stillness.

This stillness is a wonder. It is like the blue in the sky. It is vast, peaceful, and open to whatever passes through. In our efforts to deal with all our emotions and hurts and desires, we have become addicted to the emotional events of the heart and haven't realized the basic stillness inside and around our heart. It is like we have been so focused on the clouds that we forgot the sky itself.

Presence in the heart is the realization that our heart connects us to our Being. In this connection to Being, we find a sense of self which is timeless, full, undisturbed, untouched by any of our past. While the outer layers of our personal heart carry many scratches and hurts, the innermost core of our heart is as whole today as it ever was and ever will be. There is no history there.

In the Zen tradition, pure consciousness is compared to a mirror. The mirror simply reflects whatever presents itself to the mirror, but the mirror itself is not changed by anything that it reflects. The Being quality of our heart is the same thing. It just is...

In the Hebrew tradition, God is said to have revealed himself as "I am that I am."

In the presence of the heart, we find the same state revealing itself through us. We are what we are. Nobody can take anything away from that, and nobody can add anything to it either.

In the Christian tradition, the Christ is said to be born from a virgin. When we recover the sense of Being in our heart, we find that our consciousness is virgin born twenty times a day. The sense of self arises out of a virgin state of Being and the intelligence of the heart is free to emerge out of this new sense of self. As the heart's intelligence flows from beingness, it freely offers itself in an intimacy that discovers, feels, and knows whoever we are with. Including our own self.

Jacqueline brought a sense of fatigue and despair when she came.

"I'm exhausted. The doctors have checked everything and they don't know what to do with me. My alternative doctor suggested I go see a shaman. I don't want to go to a South American shaman to chase away my bad spirits. Can you help me?" she asked.

"I don't know if I can or not," I told her. "Either way, I am happy to be here with you. That's about all I can promise. Let's see what shows up."

"OK," she said.

"How big is your pain right now, and what color is it?"

"The pain feels as big as this room, or even bigger if I let it. The

color is blue."

"Tell me more about the blue, is it light or dark, heavy or light?"

"It is a lighter shade of blue, something like turquoise."

"Ok... now feel out to the boundary of this blue, as big as it is. Go just to the edge of it and tell me what you find there."

"It is very big, but I feel the edge of it as a place that is very busy. The border is very active with whatever there is around it."

"Ok...can we say that there is a lot of negotiation going on at the border?"

Jacqueline smiled. "That is a very graceful way of looking at it."

"Ok. Feel this negotiation going on, and tell me what happens in that negotiation."

"Well, the first thing is that the pain level drops about 50 per cent. I never felt friendly with the border area before, I always sensed it as some threat. Now that I am there and feeling a sense of negotiation going on, I feel like there may be something good out there which is trying to communicate with me. Strange how that idea never even crossed my mind before, but here it is."

"OK... I'm here with you now. Stay with it. On the other side of the blue border is a sense of something wanting to negotiate or communicate with you, something that might even be friendly. I would call it The Field. What happens when you let yourself relax into negotiation or communication with the Field?"

Jacqueline's whole being had shifted and her her voice had lifted. "Well, all I can say right now is that it is amazing. I don't feel myself in tension or fighting like I had been. I am relaxing into this thing you call negotiation, and I'm even beginning to like it. It is as if this Field out there is friends with me and is actually even trying to help me or support me. I'm relaxing all over. My pain is way, way down. I'm feeling light, almost like I'm weightless. I can even feel a kind of happiness in my heart. Something that I hadn't felt in this way since a long time."

"And the blue pain field?"

"It's much lighter now. Actually a very pretty turquoise, like the

water in the Caribbean ocean. It doesn't feel like it wants to carry pain or suffering. It is fresh and clean. Sparkling."

"And the rest of you?"

"I feel good. I don't know how you did that, but I feel fresh. Ready for a brand new way. Like my life is an adventure again, not some drudge."

"Stay with that," I suggested. "Just let it settle into your bones."

We sat together in stillness for another ten minutes.

Jacqueline opened her eyes and said, "Thank you. It's in my belly now. I feel full and relaxed at the same time."

In the stillness of the heart we find our deepest connection, the place where we can merge into Space and allow the consciousness (The Field) in Space to interact with our personal consciousness.

In this place we find our self to be tremendously supported, even wanted, by the universe that creates us. Not only are we wanted, but we are personally wanted, we are encouraged to manifest the unique qualities that we have brought to planet earth.

Heart Skills Summary

The heart skills are like petals on a flower. At the periphery, they look different. In the core, they all come from the same place. Heartfulness is heartfulness. It manifests in many ways, and it is more than likely that each reader can add a few more petals of heart experience to the ones we have presented already.

In the flow of the heart skills, we learn ways to approach daily living with greater skills of authenticity and love.

In the progression from the "Yes" state to the holding place to the awakening of heart intelligence and its deep capacity to discriminate, we learn a new orientation to our experience.

We learn how our heart can transform whatever it embraces. In the power of transformation we also discover the fundamental goodness that is in each of us. We learn to be confident and fearless with personal experience. This heart skill progression matures in the release of our creative power of the heart, our ability to manifest the truth of our heart.

The cycle rounds into the discovery of the silence of the heart. In the silence of the heart we feel our presence, the unique intelligence that lives in our Space. We also realize that in silence our personal presence is merged with the field of bigger Presence, the active form of intelligence that lives in all Space.

The discovery of these heartskills brings a way of renewal into the world where we feel so many challenges. They offer clear, viable alternatives to the strategies of our protection-oriented personality. They are portals out of the world of fear, struggle, and survival into a world where love and renewal happen.

Spiritual Longing

We all have a natural longing to re-connect with the wholeness out of which we come. We not only want to connect with it, but we want to live the truth of that connection in our daily lives.

In this longing, we come to face a strange paradox: we want to know God, but we are ambivalent about God knowing us. We want to know the Big Reality, and at the same time, we hardly want to know the reality of our selves.

In the Friend's way, spirituality isn't something that is practiced in a church or recovered from the depths of the Great Pyramid. Rather, spirituality is in the way we are present with our selves in our daily living.

The way we are in our body and the way we are in our heart serves as an invitation. We invite the deeper level of spiritual truth to manifest in our daily living. Sunday is a blessed day, but then again, so is Monday, and Tuesday and Saturday night.

The View

The spiritual aspiration is to re-member grace as a personal, living reality. Again, this is something like a wave remembering itself as part of the ocean.

Our spiritual aspiration is the urge to recover intimacy with the reality out of which we come. We want to live the love that brought us here. We simply want to know the truth of it. This knowing is not a philosophical foray; it is the same kind of knowing that happens between a mother and child, the knowing that comes through contact, heartfulness, and shared experiences of deep intimacy.

We remember, even if vaguely, the truth and love and light that we are in some way reaching for. We find hints of this level of being coming through in moments of quiet, lovingness, moments of totality, the experience of grace that can come from watching someone caringly put the mustard on our hot dog. We get daily postcards from the essence world — the snowflakes fall every winter — but because spiritual aspiration is connected with True Nature, we have strong ambivalence about it.

We are both attracted and repelled. We long for the grace of this world of being, yet we also have dedicated the greatest portion of our lives to creating a separate self away from True Nature.

In the normal development of child to adult, we have become heavily invested in the artificial selves that we can make and in the dream worlds that we can dissociate into whenever we feel the need for them. These survival skills we learned have protected us again and again from the harshness of socialization and sitting in a classroom at 8.30 on a Monday morning and trying to remember how many Greeks were killed in the battle of Sparta.

Our social skills protect us, tell us who we are, keep out the bad guys, keep the bad guy inside under control, give us an escape route when we need it, and give us an orientation to life that generally makes us fit into the world the way other people want us to fit in. Our social skills are state of the art systems that we have cultivated so deeply and for so long that we hardly recognize our selves when we are not using them.

We have become masters in our own way of creating realities to fit our needs and wants. Unfortunately, these fabricated alternative realities are just that...fabricated alternative realities. While Reality supports our ability to create alternate realities, it doesn't feel obligated (or sometimes even inclined) to support the truth of our illusions.

In the clear light of Reality we see that our idea to dress up the emperor in imaginary clothes hasn't given us anything more than an illusion, and that the nakedness is still exposed.

Simply put, True Nature is on a first name basis with God, while for the outer personalities, God is quite something else.

God[17] is something to be feared, worshipped, sought after, studied, thought about, and, at all costs, avoided.

For some of us, it takes a loud knock on the door to awaken our Spiritual aspiration. For others, it isn't so much a loud knock as a whisper from a lover, a moment of the heart opening into a dimension of love tenderness that suddenly feels natural and like home.

Whatever it takes, sooner or later our religious impulse wants more out of life than what it finds in the process of creating our own imaginary world, a world of buffers, protections, multiple selves, dissociations and denials.

We want something Real. Something based in Love. We want to know who we are. Why we are here. And, in some way, we yearn to know, how we can be of service.

This yearning is genuine and true.

Yet, as we know, not many people find what we really are looking for.

When we lose our connection with True Nature, we also lose the natural sensing capacity of True Nature. True Nature is still on an intimate basis with Consciousness and Creation, it is still part of the family. When we split away from True Nature, we lose our natural connection to the big field of Consciousness. We lose the eyes and ears and fingers and toes that know how to operate in the Spirit world. From behind our buffers and masks, we cannot feel and taste reality.

Our personality system is so designed to suppress the inner and activate to the outer, that we can only imagine God to be outside of us. And since we haven't met him so far, he must be Far Outside us, the ultimate object of the ultimate search.

We feel like we have to put on our best Sunday suit to go meet God, and are terrified what would happen if/when we have to undress and be known for what we really are.

Mary

The main reason the spiritual path is so demanding is that it takes us back to all the parts of ourself where we have split away. To go in search of God means to meet again the parts of us that are afraid, or hurt, or angry or lost. A common thread to all of these dis-owned pieces of self is that they became dis-owned in a time of emotional need where there was no support or emotional holding for the one in need.

In the light of this understanding, Mary is one of the best guides for the Friend's way. Mary is the archetype for the one who holds us in time of need.

Mary stands on the border of the most intimate of human experience—a mother's caring for her child—and religious experience, the place where Godliness finds its home in a human body. She is both a historical character and an archetype of consciousness which is alive and well in each of us today. Her story didn't begin or end in the Bible; her presence is as powerful and helpful today as it was 2,000 years ago.

There are many ways of seeking the divine—pilgrimages, caves, meditation retreats, church worship, personal growth projects, satsang with a Master. All of these and many more can be quite valuable.

In the Friend work, we discover another way of meeting and merging with the divine: holding the present self with tenderness and confidence.

We have learned through our journeying through water, fire, and space that the best way to know the divine is from our own personal experience. This happens as we journey through the protections we have put around our selves and come into contact with the innocent, clear core that is still inside us. This journey cannot be made by struggle and aggression. It requires humility, love, courage, and deep trust: in short it requires the kind of presence that Mary radiates.

We all have seen pictures of Mary holding the child Jesus.

Some day that child Jesus is going to be the man who became Christ, but in the meanwhile, he is still just a child.

He is not born enlightened, nor is he immune from all the things that happen to other kids who are tender and open and have to learn to live in a world that isn't very tender and isn't supporting to openness.

Mary holds him with love, warts and all. She believes in him. Somehow, by being in contact with her own grace, she is able to create a field of grace around Jesus where his grace has a chance to manifest.

Mary brings a tender, firm heartfulness in the way she holds Jesus—and us. She is that part of us that can hold our experience with love and grace, and in this love and grace, call out the true nature of who we are.

If we can learn to hold our experience the way Mary holds Jesus, we will discover the same thing happens. No matter what it is we hold, if we hold it heartfully, it will unfold in the direction of its true nature. In that unfolding flashes a clear light of intelligence: what do I discover right now? What is truly here now?

Adam came for a session about his relationship.

He said his girlfriend wanted to have a child, but he didn't. She was quite insistent on it, however, and he wasn't sure whether to continue the relationship or not.

I asked Adam how he felt about this in the moment.

Adam said, "Scared. I don't think I can even take care of myself, much less take care of anybody else."

"Where do you feel this fear?" I asked him, "How intense is it?"

He said, "It's in my belly and I would rate it at a level 7 out of 10."

I asked him, "How old is the person who is afraid?"

He said, "Uh.... about six years old. It's like the feeling I had when I was just starting school and I didn't think I was going to make it."

I asked Adam to breathe with this frightened six year old child, to

191

breathe in the fear and breathe out love to him.

Adam did this for a few minutes.

"Are you still afraid now?" I asked him.

He said, "No." His body started to tremble and he cried.

Adam said, "I'm not so much scared about going to school, I'm sad about leaving home."

I said, "Stay with that sadness. Feel it right here and right now. Breathe with it."

Adam did that.

Then I said, "You have left home a long time ago. Feel yourself now, and tell me what you have lost."

He cried for a few minutes.

"Stay with it," I said.

His breathing came slower and deeper.

"Look again," I said, "What have you lost?"

He said, "Nothing. Right now, I'm all here."

I said, "And your mother's love. You have left her physically, but is that love gone?"

He said, "No. I can still feel it around me."

"Good," I said, "Now look again. Is that love something that is in her or something that is part of you?"

Adam said, "I always thought it was hers. Right now I can see that this love is also part of me. It is not something I have to get and hold on to, it is something that I have inside and can give where I want."

He opened his eyes and said, "This is just amazing."

I said, "You've thought your whole life that love came from your mother and that when you leave her, you will lose it, and that somehow you have lost it. Now you are discovering that this love is inside of you. It is something that you can give and offer to others. You can also give it to yourself.

"So how is it for you to discover this?"

"I'm just amazed," he said, "I didn't ever realize how much love is inside me."

"In the next week, keep coming back to this place of love. Get to be

friends with it, " I said. "See what happens to this love quality when you consider whether or not to have a child with your woman."

"This is a whole different way of looking at it," he said, "I'm excited."

The ability to discover ourself is a jewel. We carry a lot of memory about ourselves and often the past is so heavy that we don't see the present. Mary's holding brings us back into the world of perpetual self-discovery. A world where what happens now is always "virgin" born and not a logical extension of what happened in the past.

What we find now recognizes a reality that is being created out of the consciousness of our present moment. We find the eyes to see things fresh, the heart that is willing to question everything, and the trust that we can let go of knowledge and return to a state of discovering.

We realize that it is not *what* we hold in our hands that matters so much, it is the *way we hold* it that is important. A child can hold a seashell in its hands and be amazed at the miracle of light sparkling on the shiny wet shell. A jaded businessman can hold a multi-faceted brilliant diamond in his hand and only think about whether it is graded as A, B, or C.

The totality and fullness that we bring to the world—to ourselves, to each other—is what reveals the miracles inside. The quality of our listening is what brings out the beauty in the music or the depth in our friend's words.

The tenderness that we offer another is the ground for hearing the tender voices coming back. The way we touch invites the body and the person to voluntarily open and share their secrets with us. To the one who has been seeking and lonely and separate for so long, these things feel like miracles.

As we learn the way of participating with others, we find that others are all too happy to participate with us.

Sooner or later we realize that the fullness of our Presence is what turns the world on.

Our Presence is like a light. What we see depends on the size and quality of the light we bring. If we bring a small, flickering light, then we will live in a world full of dark shadows and the Scary Things that live in such dark shadows.

When we bring a steady, warm light, the shadows recede. We start to see things as they are. We start to recognize the fine details in what we see, and we can appreciate the beauty of these details and the intelligence that holds all of these details together.

In some meditation traditions they say the world begins to appear as a Mandala of order, logic, and beauty when our eyes are clear enough to see it. Not only does the world appear in the beauty of a mandala, but our own being, including our history, body, heart, good, bad, all the dids and did nots, our whole story acquires a grace and beauty and logic of a mandala. The disaster of our ego's development turns into the ground for appreciating the tenderness and fullness of who we are now, and for appreciating others in the same way.

In Mary's quality of holding the self, we discover the unique, precious qualities that we are here to share. Our contribution to the earth. The exquisite love intelligence of our snowflake design, our personal mandala. We realize that we are all carrying gifts. Each of us has a sense of goodness that we want to release into the world. These things are not just static, they have a flow, a natural movement, a natural sense of expression. As we come to know and claim our natural gifts, it is easy to drop out of the old prison of who we are supposed to be and to stand fully in the light of who we actually are. We can rest in the unfolding mystery of being who we are.

Carla was raised Catholic. Now, some 45 years later, she was feeling alone, separate, and wanting to expand her ability to contact other people.

I could feel the Religious Aspiration in her as one of the dominant features of her. She was clearly what one would call a religious seeker. Seeing that this feature was so predominant in her, I knew that it would be a big ally to have in our work together.

Carla said, "I don't know what to do now. I want to work more with people and I'm scared of my own emotions. I can't get in there, and when I do, I don't like what I find."

"How is that for you?" I asked.

"I feel scared. Lonely. Stuck. And I don't like it," she answered.

"Tell me more..."

"I feel so unworthy, so small, so wanting something I will never have," she replied.

"A question for you," I said. "A strange question at first: when you are small and unworthy and unhappy, where is God?"

"He is far away," she said.

"Look again," I said. "If God is God, then he must be everywhere. And if God is everywhere, then why is he not in you? Right now, right here?"

Her eyes looked at me in wonder, then they brightened a little. "It sounds good, but I think that what you said is impossible."

"Why?"

"How can God be in me? I am scared, small, sad, and lonely. That can't be God."

"How do you know?" I asked.

"Because I was taught that God is big and happy and perfect," she said.

"Maybe He is," I answered, "and maybe that big and happy and perfect God is right now sitting right inside a woman who feels small and scared and sad and lonely."

Carla was silent for some time. I stayed in the silence with her.

Slowly she started to open her breathing, to shift out of a thinking approach into a feeling state. She was clearly wrestling with her angels and demons and I let her have the space to do so.

After some minutes, a tear came from her left eye. And then another. She took a tissue from the box on the table and held it to her eye.

"Thank you," she said. "I don't think I will ever forget this one. I never imagined that God is here in me. I always felt that I would never be perfect enough for Him."

Such unfolding goes on and on, but for now there is not much point in writing about it except to say, when you get there, you will know it.

Often clients ask me, "Where does therapy end? What is the goal of it?"

Generally, I just smile and say, "I think you will know it when you get there."

Inside myself, though, there is always a watchfulness for the Mary quality. Therapy ends when we are grounded deeply enough that we can truly hold our own experience, and in that holding find the love and intelligence of grace as it unfolds in our life.

In other words, when we have learned to be a Friend again.

Part Four

Separation from True Nature
and Returning

How We Separate From Ourselves

This section is a guide in the way we become separated from our True Nature. As we lose our contact with our most fundamental reality, we also lose contact with the fundamental reality of the world and people in which we live. We come to live in an isolation that starts in childhood conditioning and that persists and embellishes itself in adult behavior.

This story is pan cultural. It encompasses many religions, many stories of remembering some golden experience that has been since lost.

Losing Eden

We all come from a state of Being in which we are part of the conscious Being of the universe. As we manifest our individual nature out of this vast field of universal Being, we come to earth much like the snowflakes falling in the Swedish sky.

We all start as a freshly made miracle from the Grey zone, looking similar at a distance, and uniquely distinct when seen up close. As unique and as simple as any snowflake, we drift down to take our place on planet earth.

For True Nature, incarnating in a body can be a shock. We

have lost our home in timeless space and we are now located in a small, limited place. This place is a body that is helpless, often uncomfortable, and frequently (unintentionally) abused. We hurt. We are hurt. We are hungry. We are afraid. We need attention. Often the attention we get is insensitive. In the times when I was born, babies were pulled from the mother, dangled upside down and given a slap, and then put in a box in a hospital ward. Terrifying loneliness. Fear. Pain. Confusion. Inchoate communication.

We don't understand: the oneness and goodness and fullness we were living in (before the body) is suddenly lost. We don't know why. For some of us this brings a sense of rejection, and anger at the God who separated away from us. For others, there can be guilt or grief. We just don't get it.

Eden is lost. True Nature evaporates in the harsh realities of surviving in a world that we don't understand, and that certainly doesn't understand us.

Being very young and small and very dependent on the outside world for our survival, we don't have so many options available to us. Survival is our first priority. In order to survive, we have to be fed, cared for, protected, and emotionally nourished. We quickly learn that for these things to come, we have to behave in ways that encourage the Other to take care of us. We have to fit in.

Discovering and manifesting our uniqueness is hardly encouraged. Parents, teachers, siblings, friends, all have another program going... how to make us in the image that they want.

We are taught how to be "good," how to be "successful," how to be "well- behaved," how to be a member of the family and an obedient pupil. We are endlessly coached in ways to conform. Who is it that listens to us, who sees us as the individual that we are?

Being totally dependent on our coaches for our survival, we get the message very clearly: "Do what we tell you to do."

Our uniqueness and individuality and creativity are not always well received; in fact they are often punished.

We feel hurt. This hurt is intense and we feel it on a regular basis.

For a child in need of acceptance and approval, it is awful to feel shame and disapproval; in fact it is so awful that we will do anything (and I mean anything) to keep it from happening. We learn how to distance ourselves from any part of ourself that would bring disapproval and shame to us.

We can easily give other people what they want if we can just hide who we actually are.

So, for us, as well as the others around us, our natural self is often "an inconvenient fact," something that potentially separates us from others.

Survival in the Wilderness: Mind

As we grow, we develop resources for physical and social survival. One of the main resources we acquire is our mind. We can use our mind as a safe place to go when the body and environment around us don't feel safe.

In times of extreme stress, we can go so totally into the mind's imagination that we can dissociate from the physical and emotional experiences of the body. As a child can do, we simply go to a place in our mind that says, "I am not here...or, this is not me."

We learn to shut away the hurting experiences (which is why most of us remember very little of our childhood). We learn that the safest place we can go is often out of and away from the body.

As children, our intelligence is very sharp. It has to be. We are talking survival here. Very early on, our intelligence realizes that since we can't realistically change the world around us, we have to learn how to control ourselves and shut down parts of ourselves that lead to friction and pain. Learning dissociation and denial brings us a sense of safety, and strangely enough, a sense of power.

When faced with the prospect of suffering for no good reason that we can understand, we either split away from that suffering and go into the unfeeling part of the mind, or we learn to deny the suffering… just say that it isn't so, it isn't me that is getting hurt.

While the outer world is beyond our control, our inner world is very amenable. We can create whatever world we like inside ourselves, and find safety in taking refuge in that inner world. In the outer world, we are helpless. Through the mind magic of denial and dissociation, we can create an inner world where we are kings.

We can make it any way we like. We learn how to create a feeling of instant power that can rescue us from the shocks and travails of growing up. "Instant King" is powerful medicine. Easily adopted, well used, relied upon, and very hard to let go of.

Self-Creations

As we learn denial and dissociation skills, we have the tools we need to develop another socializing talent. This new talent is a further extension of the "Instant King" that we create in our inner world.

Somewhere around the age of three or four years old, we discover the capacity to create a new "Self."

As we dissociate away from the painful, "Bad," self, we have the ability to create a mask self, a happy little kid self that gives everybody just what they want. In an instant, we can magically transform ourselves from the kind of child that is being hurt or rejected into the persona that our parents want us to be.

It is a survival game. As long as we can keep up the mask, we're safe and well-liked and there's a very good chance that dinner will be on the table, warm and ready for us at 6pm.

This one is so good, that we practice it and practice it and practice it. Just imagine, if important people don't like us the way we are, then, puff! we can give them somebody else!

This style of self-management leads to our going further and further away from ourselves. In fact, after a few years, we are so familiar with our masks that we even don't remember that we are in a mask. We have fooled others into believing in these masks so much that we start to believe in them ourselves. As it is, the mask protects us, and magically opens doors to being approved, and so we have a lot of investment in them.

Our inner nature, on the other hand, seems to be a source of friction and problem making, both for us and for others. The good guy is out in front of us, and the bad guy is inside.

Losing a mask is terrifying, like being on the front lines and discovering that your sword and shield are missing. The naked exposure is absolutely terrifying. So, being the improvisational experts that we are, we learn that if one mask is threatened or not working, we just cover it with another one.

Mask upon mask upon mask gives the child the sense of greater safety and protection.

To say the word mask is not fully accurate, as what we really create are living three dimensional personality projections. We learn to create a whole synthetic self that moves, talks, thinks, has opinions, has likes and dislikes, and acts just like any other person out there. Most of the time it fools everybody else, and equally so, most of the time it even fools us.

And, throughout the remainder of our lives, as we mostly meet the masks of others, our own personal masks fit right in.

Logic and Narcissism

Around the age of six we learn another buffer system to protect us as we are socialized. We learn to find – or create – reasons. Explanations. We create a rudimentary system of logic. The ability to find or create reasons for our pain saves us from the assaults of random pain.

We create logic in our stress, and the stress becomes more bearable because it is logical. Somehow we find solace in the idea that bad things happen to us because we deserve it.

We are not yet ready to see the limitations of the people on whom we depend for our survival. For us as children, parents need to be good and powerful and somewhat just. We don't see that Daddy has had a bad day and that is why he is yelling at Mommy and that is why Mommy is yelling at us.

We see a world where we deserve to be yelled at because we didn't do something well enough to create happiness and harmony in the family.

The narcissism here is a very creative act of intelligence. What it does is take the absolute (and terrifying) helplessness that we feel, and flip it inside out to where we have a new-found sense of power.

In the narcissism of our minds, we go from being victims to being Creators. In our mind's world, everything revolves around us. "Instant King" becomes even more powerful.

In narcissism we are the center of the universe. We imagine this as a place of power and creation, where we can rationalize our emotional experience with all kinds of reasons. As creators, we then feel like we can manage the world around us by controlling our behavior.

In such a mindset, if we are good and perfect, then the family will be happy. If we are punished, it is because we deserve it, there is something wrong with us. Our deficiencies are the cause of our pain, and when we can just make our defects better, all will be well in the kingdom.

This kind of buffering works wonders for giving us a sense of an understandable world. It allows us to think of our parents as wise, just and loving beings, and to account for the family strife through our own shortcomings. Even when we are being physically or emotionally hurt, we maintain a sense of power, a sense that we are the center of the world and we are the prime cause of whatever happens in that world. We know the problem, and we know the solution: better control over our self. Life is suddenly more manageable and simple.

Over time, of course, a narcissistic attitude leads to more trouble than it is worth, something like a pair of overalls that are too tight as we outgrow them. In adults the residue becomes a something like a dark hood that we wear over our heads, even when the sun is shining. Inside this dark hood, we are living in our own separate reality.

The System

So now we have the basics, a system for coping with the wilderness outside of the Garden. We have learned the ability to make mental and emotional pain go away. We can deny, dissociate, create fictional personality masks, leave the body, and go into a mind that is our own private kingdom.

We have adopted a strong vigilance to the outer world so that we can defend ourselves from whatever slings and arrows of outrageous fortune it may have to offer. We have also learned a system of controlling our body, its life forces and its emotional reactions. This system both reduces the flow of natural impulse from the core of ourselves and maintains psychological vigilance over all our activities (real and imagined). The crowning piece of our system is the ability to shift our identification out into newly created personality masks. We can fool other people about who we are, and we can also fool ourselves.

That's it. Now we have our survival system for living in a world where we are expected to become the person other people expect us to be, for living the life we are brought up to live. This survival system I call the control system. Once this system is functional, which it will be by the age of six to eight years old, then we simply run it again and again. We tweak the settings of our control system to be more and more sophisticated, but we adapt to living inside it, the way a person would have adapted to living in a castle under siege.

We shudder to consider operating outside this control system. When we do feel painful events, we split away from the pain, and create another personality character that stands even farther out from the core than the earlier ones. This new personality character keeps getting further refined as protector and interface with the society around us.

The system is crude, but effective. Very effective. And for a helpless child in the wilderness of survival, this is truly an ingenious work of art.

The Replicating Fractals

We learn a basic operating system that saves our life as a child. When do we quit living inside it? Ask yourself or anybody else, "When did I quit doing these things?"

Sitting in the therapist's chair the answer is easy to see: we don't ever quit. We just try to build on top of it.

And therein lies the rub.

As life progresses, we become adults who maintain the survival software of little children.

While our self-management system works incredibly well for fitting into mainstream society, it has severe long term costs which only become apparent later in life.

Resources

As adults, we have a great capacity to deal with life's stresses. We have *Humor. Understanding. Love. Awareness. Wisdom. Intelligence. Compassion. Inner Strength. Insight. Meditative Presence. Arts of Defense. Skills. The Ability to Dance. To Move. To Sing. To Express. To Discuss. To Sense. To Transform. To Forgive. To Create. To Breathe. Being Curious. Being genuinely connected with True Nature.* This is a huge set of resources.

We are all truly rich beings, all of us.

Yet, because the childhood system is so set in the subconscious mind and so well practiced over the years, we don't recognize ourselves as resourceful. In times of trouble, we don't expand into our resources; we contract back into the helpless, dependent attitude of the child. In trouble, we regress into feeling ourselves to be small and helpless and unable to handle the situation. We contract, and from there we run the familiar, tried and true child survival programs.

We learned to separate out from ourselves. We learned to create buffers and buffers so that not much gets in and not much from the inside gets out. These defenses are so well known and so efficient, that we run them automatically. Instantly.

When we do this, we close down the place where our resources come from. When we dissociate, we lose contact with our body and its wisdom. When we go in denial, we lose contact with the truth inside us. When we buffer against the world, we lose our sensitivity to what we are actually contacting. When we go hyper-critical on ourselves, we lose the fluidity of our natural intelligence. When we freeze in response to the world, we lose emotional flexibility and vitality.

The dynamic, creative, inner core of true nature becomes concealed, locked away. It doesn't get the attention and exposure it needs in order to grow and mature.

We end up prisoners in our own castles. Lost to our dreams and imaginations, not ever really knowing who we are and what the world around us is.

Loss of Ground

Practicing the arts of denial and dissociation comes with a price. That price is Ignorance. We lose contact with many precious things in ourselves and also in the world around us. We operate in a field of very limited experience. We don't know our self, we suppress contact with our body and emotions, and we lose sensory awareness of both the world around us and our personal inner world.

When we see what actually happens through denial and dissociation, we recognize that they are great anesthetics, but the side effects are huge.

The victory of the control system becomes the Ignorance of the adult.

The first, and main, victim of the practice of Ignorance is True Nature.

In the effort to get away from our natural self and embrace our new artificial selves, we completely lose touch with True Nature. All the work we have done to construct a system that separates us from True Nature is successful. Our control system and personality identification systems have managed to make True Nature something we no longer have to directly experience, and have turned it into a dim, vague memory.

In effect, we are locked out of our own house.

The loss of our True Nature—more accurately said, the loss of our experience of our True Nature—is the deepest, most

207

profound loss we are likely to experience in our whole lives.

We know that something is missing; something incredibly valuable is gone. Depending on our type, there is likely to arise anger, hurt, sadness, fear, aggression, and/or dullness. Because we don't understand what is going on, we can easily blame others – our parents, society, God – for causing these awful feelings.

We compensate for this loss of our experience of the True Nature within ourselves by trying to find it somewhere else.

For the introverted types, we look for it in the creativity of our own mind. We imagine a world where we get a taste of our True Nature. We create it in artwork, in poems, in stories of mythological heroes.

For those of us who are more extroverted, we look for compensation from our social contacts, from our work, and also from our projections that can take shape in the form of many social and religious ideals. We project that other people have got something that we don't have, and we do whatever it takes to catch up.

In the loss of our contact with our True Nature, there is an undefined sense of emptiness inside. As this emptiness does not look or feel to be such a good thing, we try to avoid it, hide it, and decorate it.

Also, as this emptiness is now firmly regulated to the subconscious part of our mind, it is in that part of the psyche where we have put all the unwanted feelings that were so distressing for us. A murky floating field of bad feelings surrounds the empty place. In this murky world of bad feelings, the empty place feels like the biggest, baddest black hole of them all.

No matter what strategies we follow, we still instinctively know that we have some dark stuff hidden in our inner closets.

We can forget, but we can't escape the dark feelings and the hole of emptiness.

Having these bad things inside, and from time to time sensing the anguish of these bad things inside, gives us a strong impetus to create an even better looking personality on the outside. We don't want anyone else out there to know what we are really like, because if they did, we are sure that they would treat us in the same way that we are treating ourselves... with total rejection.

The wrongness of ourselves lurks in the subconscious, ready to spring out like germs or terrorists at any given moment. And in the center of it all is this big black hole that can suck all our good accomplishments and efforts away into oblivion.

This is not such a nice place to be. So we stay away from it as much as possible.

Losing our fundamental connection with the ground of our Being means that we are open to a whole lot of non-sense. We don't know who and what we are, so we have to guess or get the information from others. And this kind of information is rarely helpful or accurate.

When we are so separated from ourselves, we are easy victims to shame, guilt, fear... all the usual nonsense that people use to control young kids, and that, in time we learn to use to control ourselves.

Personality Parts

Another consequence of the childhood system is that we become identified with the outer layers of our personality. In that identification with the outer (created) layers of our self, we continue a system of systematically repressing the inner layers of our natural self.

The outer personality is our interface to the world. As we don't have much confidence in our distinct True Nature, we have to create an interface that makes other people happy with us.

In effect, we learn to create masks. We create a personality mask that fits one situation, and then learn to make a different mask for another.

In the process of learning the art of masking ourselves, our True Nature fragments into many pseudo-selves, many person-

ality parts. Each part is specific for a job it has to do, just like we put on one set of clothes for one activity and another set of clothes for another. We develop a whole closet of personality parts to help us get through the wear and tear of all the roles of daily life.

In time, we even get so used to putting out these masking parts that we fight within ourselves to keep them up. They are considered to be good because that's the feedback we get from others. The bigger the mask and the more dense it is, the better our chances are of making others happy and the better our chances are of fending off the pain, loneliness, confusion, sense of loss and grief we accumulate in our inner world.

As we practice the art of creating personality parts, the power of our True Nature gets transferred out into the parts we have created. The outer, created parts gradually become the self we want to be and the inner world becomes the self we are afraid of being. We naturally feed one and try to suppress the other.

In time, our personality constructions get so real, and own so much of our inner power, that we begin to live under the power of these parts.

In effect, we become victims of our own creation. That means we follow the guidance of whatever part is presently on the top of the pile. We do whatever that part tells us to do.

Such experiences keep us on a perpetual roller coaster ride.

After some time, we find ourselves truly being the victims of our personality constructions, with the personality issues being what run our lives on a day to day basis. We just do what the personality du jour tells us to do and we feel whatever emotions those personalities conjure up for us.

Our situation is very much like what Odysseus found when he finally made it back to his home in Ithaca. While he had been gone, many suitors had lined up for his wife, Penelope. All of them wanted to marry Penelope, and be declared the new king. They lived in his castle and took turns acting like a substitute for the missing Odysseus. To reclaim his wife and throne, Odysseus first had to kill or banish the imposters. To reclaim our inner being, we need to do the same thing with our personality parts.

As each layer of our "self" is created, it is further away from the living, supple qualities of the being. The being is extremely flexible and fluid, and through this open nature, it has an ease with the living matrix of the whole world.

In contrast, each personality layer is rigid. These homemade selves don't have any direct contact with the source of life, the source of goodness. They are dry and hard and vaguely aware that the ground they stand on is not very substantial. It takes a lot of energy to create and sustain the illusion of personality parts, so we are afraid that the whole part show will fall apart if we don't keep feeding them with our energy.

The insecurity of this system turns into desperate attempts to convince others that these personality parts are the real thing. We continually search for confirmation from others that, yes, we are real and "good." And, we reserve the right to get hugely upset when others don't buy into the reality of our personality parts and confirm us to be in accordance with the way we want to be. We feel hurt and betrayed and angry when we don't get the feedback that we want.

As most of us know, the desperate attempt to get confirmation from others through such things as being a nice person or getting marks in school or making money or having children or a big car or a great house... all these things, even when they succeed, leave us feeling even more empty inside. It's a hell world that we get into where if we do achieve our dream, it still doesn't give us the experience of our soul that we are looking for, and if we fail in our dream we feel miserable because of the failure. All the attempts to make this system work at best realize only short-term victories at the expense of a lot more control and effort and doing all the things that just take us further and further away from home.

In a workshop in Sweden, I asked for a brave volunteer. One woman, Inger, came forward. I asked her to stand with me in front of the group, and to place herself in the position of being the original soul of Inger and to sense its experience. With a little support, she easily fell into a place of quiet restfulness and grace. She described the love and ease she felt in this place.

Then I asked her, "What happens to this open state when it's shocked and hurt as a baby?"

Inger immediately contracted, and said, "I go into shock and panic."

I asked her, "And how was that shock and panic treated by the family around you?"

She said, "They didn't like it. They cut off from me. I felt even more alone and afraid."

I asked her, "So then what did you do?"

She said, "I hid the feelings of the hurt and created a smiling Inger that everyone seemed to like a lot."

"Good," I said."Let's ask for another volunteer to stand in the place of this new "smiling Inger." Helen came up from the group and took that place a few paces away from Inger.

I asked Helen, "How is it for you to be a smiling Inger?"

She said, "I like it because everybody loves me."

I said, "Good. How do you feel inside?"

She paused. "I feel sad. Lonely."

I asked, "What happens to smiling Inger when she feels sad and lonely?"

Helen said, "She doesn't feel like smiling so much any more, she makes a little trouble around the house so that she can get some more attention."

Another volunteer, Karin, came up to be the trouble making part of Inger.

Karin took her place and said, "I like to make trouble and do bad things, just to make things difficult for everybody else. I don't like anybody to see that, of course, but that's what I do."

Alice came up to be the cover person for the troublesome Karin. She presented herself as a smiling, quiet child that protected the trouble making Inger from being seen, and caught. Alice said, "I don't talk too much. I'm polite and do good things in school and try my best to make everybody else happy."

I asked Alice, "How old are you? How do you feel inside?"

Alice said, "I'm around 10, 11 years old. I feel very lonely and the only thing that really makes me happy is when I get good marks in school. I want mom and dad to like me, but even when they say good things about me, I don't feel much. It's like I'm hungry for something I never get."

After Alice told her story, we carried on this demonstration of a normal person's ego development—the process of adding ego layers on top of our soul.

When another five or six people had joined in, we were now working with an identity of Inger that felt close to her present age as a married mother of three kids. This new Inger stood at the end of a line of about ten different masks for the original soul.

After talking with this older, end product Inger for a few minutes, I asked her, "How does meditation look to you? What do you feel about turning inside?"

She laughed, "It is not the least bit interesting to me. I don't want to know about what is in there (here she pointed to the line of people behind her). I've got my own life to live out here," as she pointed to the *group in front of her.*

I said, "I understand. Here is a strange question for you: How do you feel about your soul? What is your connection to it now?"

She looked puzzled. "I wish I had a soul. I think I lost it a long time ago, and now I'm looking for some way to get it back. Some days I just realize I've given up on it. I hope it comes through my kids and they get to live their heart and soul. I don't know where mine is any more."

I asked the group, "Does anybody out there feel themselves to be any different from this?"

A long, deep silence settled in.

It was clear that the outer parts of the personality—our ego crust—had very little interest in turning inside. They have been created as an attempt not to feel the pain of the self. For these parts to turn back in would require some inordinate amount of stress, insight, love, or inspiration because they are convinced that the way "in" is the way back to pain, and the way "out" is the way out of pain.

These outer parts stand as guardians. They have a job to do. They are oriented to protection. Their alertness is geared to survival. Meditation for them is only acceptable if it makes one stronger and more capable of asserting one's ego in the world. Otherwise, it is more an interference than a help.

As we looked together even further into this line of personality development, the group and I saw the stress in such a system. Clearly, each ego layer feels less a sense of peacefulness and belonging. Instead, each of the outer layers is pressured by increasing angst.

This angst comes from two main sources. First is a feeling of vulnerability and failure— each layer is created because the one previous hasn't really been successful in making us happy. One layer of not being happy followed by another and yet another slowly creates frustration and hopelessness. Coincidentally, every time a new layer is created, the new layer is further from the alive, juicy, graceful soul and more and more dependent on the world outside for its nourishment, sense of self, and feedback.

As we lose contact with our innermost being, we naturally become dependent on the outside world for our sense of self. Often this means saying "no" to what is inside us so that we can say "yes" to who and what is outside.

In the end, each layer of personality adds another degree of soul denial into our experience of being ourselves.

In short, we progressively leave contact with ourselves and try to find confirmation from the world around us.

As we practice this for 20, 30, 40 years, it becomes such a deeply ingrained habit that we don't even know that we are doing it any more. We have so hypnotized ourselves into this way of being, that we can't imagine any other way of doing it.

It is no wonder that meditation and turning in are so foreign. Or that we are so hungry for the experience of our soul, but don't know how to re-unite with it.

The Split Self

A third consequence of the childhood system is that we become split into "good" and "bad" parts.

Invariably, the good parts are those parts of ourselves that skillfully bring in rewards from the outside world. The definition of "good" parts seems to be the parts of our selves that other people like.

The "bad" part of ourself is everything else. This may be the inner one, the one who has pain, who is not fully under the dominance of the control system, who may even be an aspect of our True Nature. Anything that doesn't support our control system is automatically judged to be a dangerous or "bad" part of ourself. Anyone or anything that doesn't support our ego fantasy is also dangerous. Anything that threatens our childhood coping mechanisms—whether it is internal or external—is an enemy that poses a risk of lowering our masks.

Like in the cowboy movies or the Arnold Schwarzenegger movies, the good guys have full license to do whatever it takes to keep the bad guys in their place. It can be brutal, cruel, unfair, stupid...you name it...as long as it works. Just watch a Schwarzenegger or a Bruce Willis movie and you will see how it presents the ethic that the good guy can be justifiably violent to the bad guys.

We even cheer for it, as it gives us a false sense of power that we too can have the power to subjugate inner and outer bad guys.

As we do this within ourselves, we create a system of great projections on the outside world. We project an ultimate good as being outside us. This may be pereived in the form of a nation state or a religious cause or our family or marital partner or whatever.

At the same time as we create good projections on the world, we also create bad projections on the world. We hate the opposing football team, the neighboring country, members of our own family, the devil, other religious systems, people we don't understand, things that remind us of our own pain, things which don't support our own ego defenses and the like.

A good example of our ability to project hate is the Nazi concentration camp where the "good" Germans felt totally right in brutalizing the "bad" minorities. Of course every culture has similar instances of acting out a justified sense of hate on others, even if they are a little less spectacularly efficient than the German camps.

A more modern example of the same phenomena is the ability of the American government to brutalize thousands of bad people in the name of protecting the good ones.

In such a system of separating ourselves into good and bad, invariably we try to convince others that we are good while at the same time we inwardly feel we are not good enough. Other words for "not good enough" might be bad, insufficient, genetically deficient, unworthy, guilty, a sinner, ugly, fat, and so on.

And, as we try to suppress the bad within us, we progressively separate from our True Nature and the abundant energy within it.

In order to be good, we continually monitor and restrict our natural energy. So, over time, a really good person has hardly any natural energy left! They truly do feel deficient then, and they truly do need to compensate for that deficiency with all kinds of things ranging from vitamins to personality development programs to workaholic lifestyles to religious fanaticism and political power.

In the effort to make ourselves good, we forget the ability to simply Be and feel good. Our natural value is lost, and is replaced with earned or achieved value. Since this earned or achieved value covers a deeper feeling of valuelessness, it needs to be created and re-created all the time. We have to do this, every day, like the way a sports team needs to win almost every match in order to stay on top.

In such efforting, we create an artificial world where active laziness replaces restfulness and where doing replaces being. Where simply doing nothing sooner or later drops us into deep psychological stress and fear.

In short, this splitting of ourselves into good and bad severely limits our sense of self-worth.

In the continual judgment of what is good and bad, we lose our ability to simply love. Love unites. Judgment separates. When we are cut off from our natural self, we are also cut off from the place where the uniting quality of our natural love arises. This is painful, and the reasons for this pain are so poorly understood that we try to find our way back to love by acting good and doing the right things and expecting the same thing from others.

We create a false sense of God. This false sense of God operates as though it really does know what is right and what is wrong. As we imbue this false sense of God with a great deal of power and moral authority, we come to live in our own prison of self-judgment. We are never good enough to appease our own jealous God. We are always deficient here.

For some, the pain of this situation is so acute that we simply deny it. We adopt a stubborn façade that says, "Of course I am good," and in that stubbornness we have the right to project a huge amount of guilt and negativity out on to other people. We tend to join other people who will support us in such a belief system. Such inflexibility, denial, and projection doesn't serve us well when we are coming close to the real God, so we end up in a lot of trouble here.

For others, the pain of the split self takes a more materialistic form. We learn to create artificial worlds where we can create a sense of value, and to stay very busy in these artificial worlds because they protect us from facing a larger, less forgiving world where we cannot protect ourselves so easily. We become totally identified with being a good secretary, a good official, a good wife...whatever role we can adopt. By being good in our role, then we can at least gain confirmation from others, a measure of social respectability that blunts the attacks of the inner critic.

King Arthur's story is a classic illustration of the self in its quest to be good and what happens as it denies the bad. We all fall in love with Arthur the boy who is tutored into the ways of the world by Merlin, as the chosen one who can one day pull the sword out of the stone and lead the nation back to unification. We also feel sad as, in Arthur's older age, the forces of darkness return. Led by Mordred, Arthur's illegitimate and unrecognized son, the revenge of the dark forces ultimately leads back to the dis-integration of the round table and the dishonoring of his most loyal knight and of his Queen. In the end of the story, a saddened and weakened Arthur arranges a truce between his army and Mordred's, only to see the truce broken by a snake in the grass and a knight's attempt to kill it.

Like Arthur, the self, no matter how "good" and noble it is, is always undone by its disowned elements. The disowned or excluded parts of our selves always gather power and ultimately take revenge.

Life (and who said life is fair?) is looking for unity, not the victory of the good over the bad.

It is very natural for us to cheer for the good (especially in ourselves) and denounce the bad. However, when we look a little closer into the story, we find that the story is not exactly what it appears to be. What actually happens is that the good is as violent, or even more so, to the bad, than the bad is in itself. While it is easy to catch this on CNN pictures of American troops kicking in the doors of Iraqi villagers, it is more difficult to see it within ourselves.

In the desperate attempt to be good, we don't see that the 'good' side of ourselves feels threatened by the 'bad' side. And in that sense of being threatened, there is fear, and that fear leads to violence. This fear-based violence comes out first to ourselves, second to our family and people closest to us, and third to any outside parties that reflect negatively on our opinion of how the world should be.

As children, we learned that when we are in trouble we can split off a new identity, we can create a new self that protects us from the pain and suffering of the old self. This new self will appear to be good and the old self will appear to be bad.

The newer layers do whatever is possible to keep their back to the older identities, and thus create the climate of ignorance that Gautama Buddha spoke about.

Inside the normal personality is a huge competition of different identities, each of which can be quite violent to all the other identities.

In such a field as this, true self-knowledge, or knowledge of the True Self, is nearly impossible.

The Friend's Way

The Friend's way offers a new vision of how we came to be so separated from ourselves. We are separated through the process of socialization. We have learned to turn ourselves into the people we are taught to be, and to ignore the being that we actually are.

As we learn to look inside, we can respectfully understand and handle the ego as the acquired defense system that it really is. The defense system is a series of created selves that stand before our True Nature. When we know how to address these created systems for what they are, then we can pass through them without resorting to internal violence or moral judgments. We can be 'friendly' as we go into the dark night where our soul is waiting. We can gracefully release the small, tight protection systems we are accustomed to so that we live in what we already have, the spaciousness of our being.

If we make such a journey with our eyes closed and based on old belief systems, it is a rough journey. The chances of arriving at our True Nature are practically nil. If we open our eyes and see how it really is, then we can walk gracefully through our inner architecture, and know that it will actually guide us into its inner sanctuaries. We can come into deep trust and rest while leaving no part of our self separated or left behind.

When we come through into our True Nature, we can manifest it in the world. This is the longing of our soul.

A red rose wants to be a red rose just as a white bear wants to be a white bear. We want to live our True Nature.

Once we actually know it, we can.

A Zen Koan: The Goose in the Bottle

A famous Zen Koan is told this way:

> *A man has a young goose and he puts this young goose inside a*

bottle. This bottle has a small neck and a large base, so the goose has room to grow, but no way to get out of the bottle.

The man feeds and cares for this goose, and it grows up.

Then, one day, the man wants to take the goose out of the bottle. He wants the goose to come out alive and healthy, and he also wants to make sure that his precious bottle isn't broken.

How does he get the goose out of the bottle without killing the goose or breaking the bottle?

If we transpose this Koan into the language of this book, we could summarize it this way: a man has grown up inside an ego protection system designed to keep him safe from external threats, but it hasn't left him much room to develop and get the feel of life around him. How do we get such a man out of his own bottle without overwhelming his defense systems or crushing his True Nature?

One answer to the original Zen Koan is: "Wake up! Just see it: the goose is already out. It has never been in the bottle."

This translates as: while we can imagine ourselves to be in a safe protection system such as the bottle of our own ego, in reality there is no container big enough for our real Being.

One day you just see it. At the level of Being, there is no struggle to get out of something you have never really been in. The imaginary castle of "instant King" is just that... an imaginary castle.

In the Friend's version of this koan, everyone has the freedom to find their own answer. There are thousands of true, good answers available to people who are willing to make heartful contact with the self and to follow the guidance of the self as it unfolds.

There will be many words, many languages that answer the koan, but common to all will be the smile. In that smile is the recognition that no matter what we are thinking or what we are feeling, Being and the world of grace is as immediate as the rhythm of our breath, as close as the beating of our heart.

Just see it: everyone wants to be happy.

Being is happy.

Already.

The End

Footnotes

1. Adaptation of a Sufi story told by Osho, *The Art of Dying*, Chapter 7, "The Treasure."
2. For examples of "Therapy," please see Appendix.
3. Personality is the self that we learn to be. It is our system for interfacing with people around us, the acquired, social self. We come to think of it as who we really are. I call it the created self. Presence is a quality inside each of us which is intrinsic. It is the core of consciousness that precedes any acquired sense of self.
4. Pain Body is a phrase coined by Eckhart Tolle, *The Power of Now*. It refers to the layers of the psyche where we store unconscious experiences of physical, emotional, and psychological pain. As the physical body is so intimately connected to the psyche, many present tense experiences in the physical body can trigger associations into the stored pain of the Pain Body.
5. Adaptation of Sufi Story: Mojud, the Man with the Inexplicable Life" as told by Osho in *The Wisdom of the Sands Volume 2*, Chapter 1.
6. See Appendix for section on "Myth of the Golden Childhood."
7. Appreciation to Martin Buber for *I-Thou*.
8. Adaptation of a Sufi story, "The Tale of the Sands" presented in Osho, *The Wisdom of the Sands. Vol. 1* Chapter 1
9. See *Zen Mind, Beginner's Mind* by Suzuki Roshi
10. For experience and training in Essence Breath, contact Body and Beyond.nl (www.bodyandbeyond.nl)
11. Osho, *The Fish in the Sea is not Thirsty*, chapter 4.
12. Osho, *Beyond Enlightenment*, chapter 10.
13. For experience and training in BodyFlow, please contact Body and Beyond.nl (www.bodyandbeyond.nl)

14. For experience and training in a Listening Hands approach to bodywork please contact Body and Beyond.nl (www.bodyandbeyond.nl).

15. This practice is called Tonglen. For a fuller description of it, please refer to the works of Pema Chodron, *When Things Fall Apart*, or Osho, *The Book of Wisdom Volume 1*.

16. Discrimination can be a tricky word to use in the English language, particularly in America. For many years, it was used synonymously with prejudice. Actually, discrimination is the opposite to prejudice. Discrimination is attention to the facts here and now, while prejudice is an ignoring of the facts of here and now in favor of a pre-conceived judgment.

17. In this book, the word God does not imply any specific religious affiliation or description.

Appendix

The Friend's Way to Therapy:
An example

The Friend's way to therapy focuses on feelings as a way of bringing awareness back to our self. This is a distinct shift from how we are trained to think. While thoughts are almost always outer directed and taking us into being fully absorbed in what's "out there," feelings have more connection with our inner world. For example, someone might say, "I think my neighbor is a really bad person because he lets his dog out in my yard." A therapist will take such a statement and bring it into the feeling level with a question such as, "How do you feel when the dog is in your yard? How do you feel about your neighbor?"

Answering such a question would lead to a statement such as "I feel helpless" or "I feel angry." In that kind of a statement, there is more awareness of the "I" than in the first statement where we hear the pronouncement, "my neighbor is a jerk."

In the statement about our feelings, we include ourselves more. We enter the world of subjective responding, a world where the "I" is more clearly recognized.

Thinking is the most superficial way of relating to our experience. While it may tell us a lot about what we imagine to be out "there," it doesn't really include us. Feeling the world is a deeper way of relating, and it begins to include our self in relation to whatever it is that we are feeling. It recognizes the truth of the relating.

This is a really big step, and it often takes years to fully develop. It takes a lot of practice to recover the ability to recognize what we are really feeling, especially when our thinking machines are running full time.

While recognizing what we feel is a big step into our inner world, the exploration stays shallow if we only sense our feelings and don't go deeper. Just sensing feelings takes us into a world where we feel a lot, but it also leaves the impression that we are the victims of a whole lot of feelings and that our job is to somehow cope with all the feelings that come to us on a daily basis.

There are no deep resolutions here, just a lot of movement. In our world of the Friend, therapy leads to an awareness of who is having an experience. Who is angry? Who is sad? Who feels lost? Who wants a better job?

These kinds of questions often catch us by surprise. We are so used to bringing all our attention to what we experience, that we completely lose track of who is having this experience.

Let's say that Dave has come for a session, and in the session he says, "I am upset with my boss."

It would be natural to ask, "What would you say to your boss if you were really free to do that?" or "Take this pillow in your hands and pretend that it's your boss...what happens?" These things invite Dave to explore the repressed words and energies he has with his boss, but they focus on Dave looking out at his boss and they neglect turning back in and also looking at Dave.

For turning in, I use a different approach. Here I would say, "How is it for you to be upset with your boss? How is it for you to be having this experience?" Here the focus shifts into a different dimension, away from the boss and back to the one who is having the experience.

Often that opens the eyes to a whole new way of perceiving the situation: How am I with this quality of being upset? Is it Ok for me to be upset? How do I handle this experience?

If we can stay there patiently for a while, it slowly dawns that "I" am the one who is having the experience of being upset, yet the upset and the I are not the same thing.

This is a major breakthrough. When Dave came into the

session, there was no difference between him and being upset. He was upset. Now he is aware that upset is something he experiences, but that he is bigger than this experience. In effect, he is handling it rather than it is handling him as he originally thought.

Once the attention comes back to our self, another question soon follows: "Who is this Dave that is having this experience?"

From his report, it's clear that a lot of strong things are being felt. Who is creating and evaluating this feeling?

As relating with ourselves this way is somewhat unusual, I often start with simple questions that make it more tangible. Frequently I ask the age. "How old is this person who is upset with the boss?"

This invites Dave to feel "who" is upset. In most emotionally charged situations, that "who" is not a 42-year-old mature adult male, but is a far younger person. You can feel this difference by asking the age.

Dave might wiggle in his chair a little here, but when he feels supported he will say something like, "I guess around 16." (It could be 10 or 6 or 4…)

I'll ask, "What's it like for this 16 year old Dave?"

"I'm feeling very alone in the world and I'm looking for my father and some support but I don't get it and I'm also rebellious and angry. I hate my father because he can't really help me and all the things he says aren't helpful for my life."

Here we are discovering what I call an "Identity." Identities are like hidden pieces of our Self that have been split off.

With Dave's 16 year old, the identity is someone in trouble. And, because we couldn't find a solution for them, we separated ourselves away from them. I often say, "We locked them in the closet."

When you work deeply with people, you will likely find many such identities. All kinds of lost, angry, sad children, hopeless teenagers and the like. If you are a bodywork therapist, you will find that the identity in the arm is much different from the identity in the leg. And they are both strangers to the one in the belly.

Each identity has a story to tell. Each has a feeling that cries to be felt. Each has its own agenda. One will be angry, another will be sad, and a third will be perpetually cheerful. These different identities jostle with each other for capturing our attention and claiming the title of "The Real Self."

When we are not aware of what's going on, we become totally identified with the identity of the moment, and see the world from its point of view. We totally believe that this is how things are. Without looking back in at ourselves, we, like Dave, think that it is "me" who is so angry with the boss.

We have no idea that it's just a piece of me that is serving us this experience, and that different pieces of us would report different experiences.

In being so identified with a single point of view, we lose contact with the rest of us which has many bigger, alternative points of view.

In Dave's case, seeing the boss from the point of view of a frustrated 16 year old boy is certain to bring in feelings of being upset. Without the ability to "turn in," Dave will be convinced that he is upset. He doesn't know that he is experiencing his boss from the projection of a 16 year old.

If Dave has some experience with therapy, I may ask him, "As you feel this frustrated 16 year old, take a moment to breathe with him and then drop into the layer underneath.... what is there?"

It is immensely helpful to drop two or three layers into each experience, and discover that under the 16 year old identity there may be a 12 year old, or a 6 or 3 year old or even someone in the womb. All of them have a different perception of the world and a different story to tell. It is like going into an archeological dig where one city has been built on top of another and another.

In such dropping down, the relativity of each layer becomes very clear. When Dave is in his 16 year old, he is convinced that this is the "real" Dave. If he were to drop into the 12 year old layer underneath, that layer would feel more "real" and be experienced as more true. Its emotional intensity would be stronger. If Dave were to keep dropping we would come into further layers where the defenses were not so well constructed and the raw, open, needing, asking parts of himself were even more apparent. Each of these would feel more real than the layer above it.

Each layer holds a fragmented identity and each has a story to tell, and feelings to feel, and lessons to be learned. From the point of view of the Friend work, however, the most important things are the discovery of the relativity of an identity, and the ability to be with an identity without unconsciously assuming that it is the real person that we are.

Appendix Two

Inner Architecture and Buddhist insight

Inside each of us is a psychological system with its own architecture. The Friend's work has shown that navigating the inner architecture is challenging, but very possible when we have the keys to open certain doors inside.

The master key, of course, is love. If we can love our inner barriers, then they respond to the quality of love that they feel.

In my experience as a therapist and meditator, I've often come across what the Buddhist tradition calls "Ego." In the meditator's tradition, Ego is a poison which keeps us locked into past oriented karmic behavior. It is an ugly phenomenon replete with monsters and demons and behavior patterns which will land us in Hell.

In the light of western psychology, a new light on ego emerges: ego is a protection system that comes from early childhood times. As it worked to protect us when we were small and helpless, we continue to rely on it for the rest of our lives. In so doing, we continue to operate in the emotional conditioning of a helpless, young child, and miss the opportunity to live from our adult, present resources.

When we look at ego as a monster, we are likely to fight it. If we look at ego as a child's protection system, then we can acknowledge it, and relate with it with love and understanding. In my experience, the latter is a master key for moving through the ego defenses that have bedeviled meditators for hundreds of years.

To come to this point of view, we need to challenge part of Buddhist mythology. Namely, that Buddha had a golden childhood.

The Myth of the Golden Childhood

In the Buddhist tradition, Gautama Buddha was said to have been born and raised in the most wondrous of places. He had a golden childhood. Raised by a king and his beautiful wife in a bejeweled palace, Siddhartha was granted his every wish and ran freely in a kingdom devoted to his wellbeing.

It wasn't until he became an adult that he encountered the reality of suffering and the forces of Mara (illusion) that are heavily invested in keeping suffering going.

As he approached enlightenment, these forces challenged him until he emerged victorious. Out of his awakening, Buddha brought forth one of his foundational, noble truths: "Life is suffering."

If we look at this story from a Western psychological point of view, we see that the myth of the golden childhood covers some very basic facts of how children come into life on planet earth.

The Siddhartha story glosses over the reality of childhood pain, fear, contraction, identity building and such. It makes childhood into a fairytale, and as soon as it does that it misses the foundation of where Ego comes from. Even the sons and daughters of Noble birth go through very painful childhood conditioning. When we don't know where Ego comes from, then we view the Egoic behavior of people as <u>adult</u> behavior.

In the Buddhist psychology, neurosis boils down to a core of three "Poisons:" Desire, Hatred, Ignorance. These poisons are viewed as manifestations of a deranged adult mind acting under the karmic influences of other lives. Buddhists tend to act as if these three poisons emanate out of the moral functioning of adults. Maybe they do, but equally likely is that the roots of Desire, Hatred, and Ignorance are in the emotional conditioning we got as children. Desire, Hatred, and Ignorance make a lot more sense when they are viewed as adult compensations for childhood fear and alienation.

Buddha taught, "Life is suffering," but Buddhists never

realized the connection between the supposed golden childhood and adult suffering. By maintaining the myth of the golden childhood, we can't see into the conditioning process that happens for each child.

Life is suffering if you suffered as a child, built defenses around this suffering, and live the rest of your life maintaining these antiquated defenses and the trapped identities inside them. Yes, that is suffering. But when we release defenses and identities and recover our basic consciousness, life is not suffering. Then life is actually quite exquisite.

The *denial* of childhood suffering is what makes suffering appear to be a universal statement on the human condition. In reality nobody has a golden childhood. Nobody. The reality of our childhood conditioning means we have suffered, that we have created protections against further suffering, and that we will internally cling to the identity of our suffering child until we wake up to the facts and release it.

These things are facts, not our enemy. If we learn to recognize the child's patterns within us, then ego is not seen as deficient adult behavior, it is a repetitive protection system of a hurt child.

When we recognize the hurt child within these repetitive protection systems, then our perception of ego changes. We understand it in a different light. In this different light it is easy to open the heart to ego, and in that heartfulness with ego, ego also responds.

The Tibetan prayer flags outside my window endlessly flutter their message in the Dutch winds: "May all beings be Happy." It is my wish that the Friend's understanding of ego will serve those whose meditation and devotion has brought so much clarity to this world already.

May all beings be Happy.

BOOKS

O is a symbol of the world, of oneness and unity. In different cultures it also means the "eye," symbolizing knowledge and insight. We aim to publish books that are accessible, constructive and that challenge accepted opinion, both that of academia and the "moral majority."

Our books are available in all good English language bookstores worldwide. If you don't see the book on the shelves ask the bookstore to order it for you, quoting the ISBN number and title. Alternatively you can order online (all major online retail sites carry our titles) or contact the distributor in the relevant country, listed on the copyright page.

See our website www.o-books.net for a full list of over 500 titles, growing by 100 a year.

And tune in to myspiritradio.com for our book review radio show, hosted by June-Elleni Laine, where you can listen to the authors discussing their books.

MySpiritRadio